COLLECTING
World Sea Shells

COLLECTING

World
Sea Shells

by Alan Major

Illustrations by Barbara Prescott
photographs by Tom Scott

JOHN BARTHOLOMEW & SON LTD
Edinburgh

Dedicated to my parents,
Ann and Percy Major,
who endured my childhood naturalist years
when I kept all manner of 'creepy-crawlies'
in bottles and tanks in the house.

© Alan Major 1974
First published 1974
by John Bartholomew and Son Ltd.
12 Duncan Street, Edinburgh EH9 1TA
Also at 216 High Street, Bromley BR1 1 PW
ISBN 0-85152-936-4

Designed by Youé and Spooner Ltd.

Filmset by Filmtype Services Limited, Scarborough
Printed in Great Britain
by Morrison and Gibb Ltd.
London and Edinburgh

Contents

Acknowledgments

The publishers are grateful for the assistance of David Heppell, Keeper of Conchology of the Department of Natural History, The Royal Scottish Museum, Edinburgh, who kindly supplied the subjects for the colour photographs and also to Tom Scott whose excellent photography shows the natural beauty of those shells.

The author wishes to express his thanks to Barbara Prescott for her co-operation and advice during preparation of her skilled illustrations to support the text.

Lastly, but by no means least, acknowledgment of thanks is made to his wife for reading and checking the proofs with the author.

LIST OF COLOUR PLATES

Author's Introduction

Shell collecting is not a new hobby. Two centuries ago rich men vied with each other to buy for their collections the exotic shells brought back from remote places by the crews of ships. In the Victorian period it was customary for the wealthy to have a cabinet of shells as part of the furniture, in which shell specimens were displayed. Little interest was taken in the living molluscs, or how they created their home; only in the shells themselves. These were regarded as 'curiosities' and the more incredible and strange they were in shape the more highly prized and valuable they were.

In recent years there has been a renewed interest in shells, and collecting them is within reach of everyone. Perhaps most collectors begin by walking on a shore, discovering and picking up a particularly colourful or wonderfully shaped example. They take it home and on their next visit add more, and so on. It is an interest that can be continually sustained by new additions, because shells vary widely in shape, size and colour. There are up to 100,000 kinds of marine molluscs throughout the world, about 600 of them being found around Britain's coastline. Thus a good general collection can be made, or the collector can specialise in one group, i.e., the Bivalves, or only one family, for example, the Cones or Conches.

My book has several purposes. Firstly, it is intended for the holidaymakers who stroll casually on the shore, either in the British Isles, Europe, the Mediterranean countries or the United States, picking up an accumulation of shells which they take home as mementoes, and then find they need a book on the subject to help to identify them. Their interest satisfied, these semi-collectors may then become full-time enthusiasts. This book not only describes the various species of shells, the shore zone to visit and the type of habitat to search, i.e., rocks, sand, etc., but also tells how to collect, the equipment required, how to deal with the gathered shells, and how to store them. Secondly, the book is intended as a reference for the serious collectors, both in the British Isles and United States, who need to know more about the molluscs of each other's country.

European and Mediterranean species are also included for the same reason. This is especially useful to those collectors who correspond with collectors in other countries and swap shells by mail. In this way a valuable and interesting collection can be built up. Shell clubs are also being widely established, where you can swap your shells or arrange to swap with members of clubs in other countries. If you do any swapping always remember to let the other collector have as much data as possible about the specimens you are sending.

Shell shops, which sell shell specimens from all over the world, are becoming increasingly popular, not only in seaside resorts, but also in towns and cities. Here shells may be bought solely as souvenirs, or the serious collector can add to his collection by obtaining new specimens.

Another purpose of my book is to help identify and give background information about the majority of the shells available in these shell shops. This is necessary because most of these shops put only the name and country of origin on the shells they sell.

Lastly, I must add a few words about conservation. If the shell picked up casually on the shore is empty the mollusc has died and so the shell can safely be collected. However, when specimens of living molluscs are being obtained for their shell care must be taken. NEVER take every specimen you find in the habitat. ALWAYS leave several to continue the species. If all are selfishly removed then it is quite obvious that eventually the species will die out in the habitat and maybe along the entire coastline. Also, try to leave the habitat as you found it. For example, if you have overturned any rocks in your search, please put them back in their proper places. Remember, other people visit the shore just to see its wild life inhabitants and not to collect. There is no place so dismal as a barren habitat, where once species were prolific. The existence of marine molluscs, as much as other forms of natural life, is threatened by pollution and various types of destruction, and they need wise and careful husbanding by collector and conservationist alike. Then there will always be good shell hunting.

Thanington, Canterbury Kent.   ALAN MAJOR

Glossary
of Words Used In Shell Descriptions

Adductor Muscle A powerful anterior or posterior muscle which attaches the bivalve mollusc to the shell wall and holds it firmly in position. Its ends are securely fixed to the valves closing the shell by contraction, pulling the two valves tightly together.

Adductor Muscle Scars The sites on the interior of empty bivalve shells, one or two scars or depressions, where the adductor muscles were attached.

Anterior The front end of the shell. The curved beaks of some shells point in an anterior or forward direction.

Aperture The entrance, opening, or 'mouth' of gastropod shells.

Apex The tip or summit of the shell, which was first formed by the mollusc. With Limpets it is the pointed crown; in bivalves both valves' beak or umbo; in the coiled univalves the small first or top whorl of the spiral.

Apical Description of the whorl shape at the tip or apex of coiled gastropod shells.

Apophysis A protuberance or projection beneath the beak of rock-boring Piddocks; the curved prong of Common and Blunt Gapers.

Beak The curved, protuberant, usually pointed, apex tip of a bivalve shell valve. Also called the umbo (See Umbo).

Body Whorl The lowest and bottom coil or whorl of a gastropod shell, nearest the aperture and sometimes the widest part of the shell.

Byssus Fibres or 'threads', produced in bundle-like growths from a gland in the 'foot' by certain bivalve molluscs, such as the Common Mussel, to fix themselves to rocks, piers, breakwaters, etc. Sometimes called the beard.

Callus The gastropod's thickened lip of the aperture.

Canal A groove in the lip or extension of the aperture's margin of a gastropod shell where the siphon protrudes.

Cancellated Marked with cross-lines, ribs and intersecting ridges; reticulated.

Cardinal Teeth The central teeth part of the jointing of bivalve shell hinges.

Carinate Keeled or angled.

Chondrophore A pit or projection in the beak or umbo of a bivalve shell where the internal ligament is attached.

Cingulated Ornamented or sculptured in a spiral manner.

Columella The axis or central pillar of a gastropod's shell, surrounding which the shell's coils or whorls spiral.

Columella Muscle The muscle which attaches the gastropod to the columella. When relaxed the gastropod is extended, but when the muscle contracts the gastropod is withdrawn inside its shell.

Convoluted The bottom or outer whorl of a gastropod's coiled shell; it hides the inner whorl and thus does not have an umbilicus.

Costa, Costae Terms for rib and ribs.

Crenated Notched, toothed, scalloped edge or edges.

Crenellated Notched, indented.

Crenulated Notched or scalloped.

Decollated Shells where the apical whorls are broken off or worn away.

Dextral A coiled gastropod shell which is 'right-handed', with the spiral winding clockwise from the apex to the aperture. If the shell is held with the spire upwards and aperture towards the person it will be seen that the aperture is on the right side of the spire.

Ears Lateral projections on both sides of the beak or umbo of a Scallop, where the elastic-like ligament holds the two valves together. Sometimes also called the wings.

Epidermis The outer layer, skin or cuticle; applied to the eggs of molluscs. Formerly and incorrectly used to describe a shell's outer layer or periostracum.

Equilateral Having all sides equal. Used to describe bivalves if the two shells, in front of and behind the beak or umbo, are same size and shape. The reverse is inequilateral.

Equivalve Used to describe bivalves if the two shells are similar in size and shape. The reverse is inequivalve, where one valve is larger or differently shaped than the other valve.

Front end Self-explanatory, but for the collector to distinguish the front end from the hind end of a bivalve it should be held with the shell hinge uppermost and the beaks or umbones directed forward. The lunule is in front of the beaks or umbones and the ligament lies behind the beaks or umbones while the pallial sinus and siphons are at the rear of the mollusc.

Gape The space between the valves in certain bivalve species after they have been closed.

Growth lines Axial lines or blemishes, irregular in shape, caused by stoppages in creation of shell.

Heterodont Term for teeth on bivalve hinge which are not uniform and differ from each other. There are several variations of these dentitions. (See Taxodont.)

12

Hinge The position where the two valves of the bivalve are jointed for articulation.

Imbricated Overlapping in an arrangement like roof tiles.

Imperforate Without an umbilicus opening or depression.

Inner lip The aperture's inside margin from the columella's or central pillar bottom to the suture or spiral line formed by the junction of the gastropod shell's whorls.

Involuted The bottom or outer whorl of a gastropod's coiled shell hides the inner whorl but it does have an umbilicus.

Lateral teeth The supplementary teeth on each side of the bivalve's central cardinal teeth.

Left valve A bivalve's shell on the left of the mid-dorsal line.

Ligament The flexible, elastic, external or internal band of fibrous tissue that hinges the bivalve's two valves or shells together; it is sited behind the beaks or umbos. If it relaxes, perhaps on the death of the mollusc, the two valves separate and gape wide.

Lip The gastropod shell's aperture margin, which may be thicker than other parts of the shell. The lip has a groove or notch (See Canal) where the siphon is protruded.

Lunule A depression in certain bivalves, long, triangular or heart-shaped, sited in front of the beaks or umbos and normally a different colour from the remainder of the shell area.

Mid-dorsal line The coiled gastropod's spiral, half-way between the sutures; the bivalve's hinge line.

Nacre The irridescent, pearly, deposit lining the inside of the shell of various molluscs; mother-of-pearl.

Nacreous layer One of the three layers of a shell, the deepest, formed of nacre.

Outer lip The gastropod aperture's outer margin from the columella's or central pillar's bottom to the suture or spiral line, which may be thicker than other parts of the shell. The margin of the body whorl opposite the inner lip.

Pallial line A line on the inside margin of a bivalve shell, joining the two adductor muscle scars, showing where the mantle edge was sited while the mollusc was alive.

Pallial sinus An inward curve or notch of the pallial line, opening close to the posterior adductor muscle scar; shows the site of the siphons while the mollusc was living.

Parietal lip or wall The part of the inner lip of a gastropod which is thickened and sited in the parietal region. The latter is an area of the aperture on the columella side, opposite the outer lip, which forms a portion of the last or bottom whorl.

Pelecypod A bivalve.

Perforate Having an umbilicus.

Periostracum The outer, horny, sometimes fibrous, layer of a shell, which is frequently worn away by the action of the sea moving the shell against another surface.

Peristome A gastropod shell's aperture rim.

Periphery A whorl's widest part, projecting the furthest distance from the axis.

Pillar Former name used by conchologists for the columella.

Protoconch The first apical whorls or part of a gastropod shell, having a different colour, pattern or outline to the following whorls; formed during the embryonic or larval period of the mollusc. In bivalves called the prodissoconch, the small first shell on the beaks or umbos.

Radial The sculpturing or colour pattern which runs from the beak to the outer margin of the bivalve shells.

Ribs The raised areas above the surrounding surface, running vertically in gastropods and radially in bivalves and the Limpets. Also called the costae.

Ridges The raised areas above the surrounding surface that run spirally in gastropods and concentrically in bivalves and the Limpets.

Right valve A bivalve's shell right of the mid-dorsal line.

Scalariform Where the whorls are not joined but created in a loose spiral as if stretched apart.

Sculpturing Raised pattern on a shell's surface.

Sinistral A coiled gastropod shell which is 'left-handed', with the spiral winding anti-clockwise from the apex to the aperture. If the shell is held with the spire upward and aperture towards the person it will be seen that the aperture is on the left side of the spire. (See Dextral.)

Siphonal canal See Canal.

Spiral Sculpturing which circles each whorl parallel to the suture.

Spire The whorls of the coiled shell, from the apex at the top, except the largest and bottom whorl.

Striae Narrow, lengthwise grooves, marks or stripes.

Striation The arrangement of the striae.

Suture The continuous spiral line of a gastropod shell created by the adjoining junctions of the whorls.

Taxodont Used for bivalves that have numbers of similar small teeth on the hinge, alternating with sockets.

Teeth Not food-obtaining in this sense, but the hinge's projections that joint the two valves of a bivalve.

14

Truncated Shortened, as if lopped off; with spiral shells the apex may be worn or broken off.

Umbilicus An opening in coiled gastropod shells at the bottom of the spiral, not to be confused with the aperture; a depression of the gastropod shell on a part of the body whorl, the columella in this case being hollow.

Umbo, Umbones The area of a bivalve shell sited behind the beaks, but also used in descriptions to include the beaks. (See Beak.)

Varix An axial rib or 'false lip', formed by the mantle edges, thickened during a retardation or pause in the rate of growth during the development of the gastropod shell. Sometimes caused by fluctuating temperatures in the mollusc's habitat.

Ventricose Bulbous or swollen whorls.

Whorl A spiral gastropod shell's complete visible single coil. The penultimate whorl is the smaller whorl above the body whorl; the body whorl is the largest and bottom whorl, with the aperture, etc.

1   How to Collect

Shell collectors are fortunate, because they can pursue their hobby without having to buy costly or elaborate equipment. Some of the basic items required can be improvised.

As a temporary container for shells collected on the shore take a strong flat-bottomed wicker basket with a handle in the centre. A shopping basket would do. To the base screw some wood cross-pieces, to act as a protective stand when the basket is continually placed on rock surfaces.

The interior of the basket should be divided up – plywood will be suitable – into varying-sized compartments in which the shells can be placed to prevent them tumbling about as the basket is carried. The shells can be placed in plastic bags to keep the basket reasonably clean. Alternatively, the compartments can all be made the same size and jars placed in them to hold the living specimens. The jars should have tight-fitting lids or screw tops with rubber washers. On top of the lid or on the side of each plastic bag stick a piece of gummed paper or adhesive tape.

Obviously, as the number of shells collected on an excursion increases some means must be used to know when and where they were found, otherwise on returning home all will be confusion trying to remember these details.

On the lid label write with biro, pen or black pencil a letter or code number. In a pocket notebook write the same letter or code number and alongside it give the necessary details – locality or zone, the habitat, i.e., sand, rocks, debris, alive or empty, date and time.

In addition to the basket, or as an alternative, a haversack with a strap that can be worn across the shoulders is useful. This can hold either the very large shells, put in plastic bags and numbered, which do not fit into the basket's jars or compartments, or small tins or boxes, filled with cotton wool, for fragile specimens, and plastic or glass tubes used to hold the very small shells.

A cardboard box is another way of carrying a haul of shells but it soon becomes soggy through being placed on the wet sand and rocks and therefore is not entirely satisfactory, particularly if the bottom drops out before the collector reaches home!

It is advisable to wear a pair of strong, ridge-soled sandals or shoes. Not only do these give protection against the sometimes extremely sharp-edged shells, spined marine creatures and fish that lie in mud and sand, but they also allow the collector to get a better grip on the rocks when climbing on them. Bare-footed, this can be a painful and hazardous experience. The wearing of rubber gloves, with the surface roughened with glasspaper, is a good idea when searching in rock crevices, sand and pools, where it is not known what might be lurking there. The roughness on the glove fingers helps you to grip rocks when climbing.

To prise Limpets carefully from rock surfaces a penknife or spatula should be taken. A table knife or glazier's putty knife will serve the same purpose. The really tight-clinging species may need a hammer and chisel but this is not recommended as they usually damage the shell margins.

A garden spade will be needed to dig out some of the living bivalves, such as the Razor Shells and Cockles, from the sand. If one is seen disappearing into the habitat dig rapidly alongside the mollusc's position and it may work its way into the hole you have made. Digging above it might mean you will strike the shell with the spade and damage it. Another idea is to take a small mesh sieve and put in it the sand you have dug out with the spade. This might help to trap the mollusc before it digs itself down too deep. The sieve, if it has a handle, can also be used to trap swimming molluscs as they pass by. Also useful is a plastic bucket into which the shell and muddy sand can be put with water to wash the specimen clean.

Another useful item for looking into rock pools or below the surface in shallow parts of the sea is a glass-bottomed wood box. It does not have to be very large; eight inches by six inches is a handy size. It is particularly useful when the wind is continually disturbing the water's surface. If held so that the glass is just below the surface the collector has an undisturbed view of the sea bed or pool bottom, and can see if there is anything to collect.

By walking to the tideline it is often possible to find numerous shells or shell fragments. This may be how many collectors begin their hobby, after noticing and picking up a particularly colourful specimen. These empty shells of dead creatures, however, may have been drifted back and forth on the shore by the tide for a considerable time and so are usually in a poor condition, with the periostracum worn away and shell surface scratched and pitted. To secure as perfect as possible shells for a collection the living molluscs must be obtained. To do so study first their life story and the especial habitat on the shore where they may be discovered, as the various species frequent different levels or zones.

These zones are known as the supralittoral, upper, spray or splash zone; the mid-littoral or middle zone; and the sublittoral or lower zone.

The supralittoral or upper zone is that area of the shore which extends from the highest level reached by the highest tides – the equinoctial spring tides in March and September – down to the average highest level of the ordinary fortnightly spring tides. On its inland side, as two of its names indicate, particularly where there are cliffs or high rocky coastline, it has a spray or splash zone, where the pounding of the surf at high tide splashes the coast with spray.

The mid-littoral or middle zone is the shore area from the base of the supralittoral or upper zone, the average high water level, down to the average low water level of the neap tides. This zone comprises most of the shore and each day is twice uncovered to the air and twice submerged by the sea.

The sublittoral or lower zone is the area descending seawards from the mean low water level of neap tides down to the shore limit at the extreme low water level of spring tides. This zone is usually covered by the sea, except during the spring tides.

Of course, there are variations in the times when low water of spring tides occurs and to discover them local tides tables should always be consulted before visiting an unexplored shore.

The extent of the high-water mark, the limit reached by the tide on that particular part of the coast, is indicated by the strand line, a line of seaweed, dead marine creatures, refuse and debris left by the receding tide. Another indication of high-water mark may be the shape of the shore, the high-water mark ending where the slope of the shingle ends and the more level beach of pebbles and dry shingle begins. Yet another indication of high water is the row of green, yellow and black lichens along the length of the lower cliff, below which the saltness of the sea has discoloured the cliff. Below the line seaweeds may also be attached. Advice should always be taken about those parts of the coastline where the unwary can be cut off by the incoming tide.

The species and numbers to be found depends on the type of shore, but no shore should be neglected just because it might look unpromising. The opposite may be the case, although no doubt some shore types are better than others.

Shingle is the most barren habitat for shells, because the material is continually being moved and pounded by the sea. Here all that can usually be found are shell fragments of species that were originally cast up from a greater depth.

On firm, soft, fine or coarse sandy shores there will also be a large number of shell fragments or shells in poor condition but few collectable examples, except perhaps after a storm when better specimens are driven inshore. On the sandy shore it will be necessary to use the spade to dig for living specimens buried at varying depths.

Muddy sand or mud may also have some shells of dead creatures on it, but within it, living on the deposit of organic matter, there are a considerable number of molluscs. Estuaries and their mudflats can be particularly rich in species.

The shore with a mixture of flat and variably-shaped and sized rocks and varying depth pools probably provides the best hunting and most excitement, because in this type of habitat exists an abundance of species. There is always hope of something especially good being found in the next pool or clinging to the next boulder. Seaweed-strewn rocks are particularly favourable as they provide shelter for numerous univalves.

There are also combinations of these types of shore, rocks with sand or mud, shingle and sand, pebbles and muddy sand, rocks and clay, mud, sand and gravel and others, either mixed or in separate but close areas, all of which have species that have adapted themselves to their particular habitat. It must also be remembered that species of univalves and bivalves can also be found when revealed by the retreating tide attached to break-waters, pier piles, jetty walls, wrecks and other objects on the shore. Generally, univalves are found attached to rocks because their shape can resist the pounding action of the sea, whereas bivalves are beneath the safer surface of the sand and mud.

Most shell collecting takes place during daylight at low tide, by walking the shore, examining the rocks and other habitats. In most cases, except in rock pools, the living species will be hidden and dormant, awaiting the return of the water. At night in shallow water, as the tide turns, if the collector treads carefully, these will be seen actively progressing and feeding, far more than the collector perhaps imagined were present in the area. To see them the collector should carry a hurricane or storm lamp or a handled battery torch. If the familiar battery torch without a handle is used, preferably with a rubber or plastic casing, leather straps can be fixed around it so it can be buckled to an arm, thus ensuring that the light shines on the shell as it is being picked up, leaving the hands free to do so. Or a length of cord can be tied to the torch to make a loop so that the cord is hung on an arm and held and released as necessary. Both methods ensure that the torch does not have to be put in the pocket or haversack every time two hands are needed to gather a shell, thus plunging the sea and collector into darkness, and also avoids accidentally dropping the torch into the water.

There are numerous species of molluscs which never venture

into shallow water, unless driven there by a storm or the sea's movement after death. Collectors who are also skin-divers and sub-aqua enthusiasts can venture into the deeper water beyond the extreme low-tide limit to obtain species that lie, sometimes widely scattered, on the sea bottom. Here all that may be needed are a net bag to contain the shells and a knife to prise off rock-clinging species. A handled sieve can catch passing species as they swim along. Wear protective gloves and shoes or sandals. Shell collectors who own, or can hire, a boat can also obtain these sea bottom species by using a dredge. There are various types. One is conical in shape, made of tough canvas with an iron lip to strengthen it, to which is attached the towing chain. Another is bag-like in shape, made of strong netting, joined to an iron rectangular frame, about two feet wide at the mouth, and having curved upper and lower flanges. The depth of the water should be estimated and a length of line approximately three times this figure should be secured to the dredge. The boat should be moved forward reasonably slowly; if too fast the dredge will be towed clear of the bottom and nothing will be obtained; also, the dredge may hit an underwater obstruction and be damaged or lost. By holding the hauling rope for a few seconds it can be judged from the vibration whether the dredge is working on the sea bottom. The conical type dredge is better for obtaining sand and mud, from which a variety of shells may be removed by washing it in a bucket. The bag-like netting dredge collects the larger shells but allows the mud and sand to filter away while being towed. Stones, rocks, pebbles, large seaweeds and debris are also certain to be gathered. These should be examined before returning to the sea because molluscs may be attached to them.

The preservation of the shells, particularly those of living molluscs, should be done as soon as possible after reaching home. If delayed, the molluscs may die and decompose, so that the task will be at best smelly and unpleasant.

Shell collectors vary in their opinions concerning the best way to kill the living mollusc in its shell. One method is to drop the mollusc into boiling water, which kills it almost immediately. The time the mollusc remains in the water has to be judged carefully, depending on the species. Generally the small species need a few seconds but larger molluscs approximately 15 minutes. The risk is that if given too long the univalve mollusc may be 'cooked', and in this condition can be more difficult to remove from its shell. The boiling water can also split some thin, delicate, shell species or 'craze' the surface of others and spoil their appearance. The second method is to put the living species in water that is fast coming to the boil and remove them as soon as the water does so. The third method is to boil the water first and as it cools place the living molluscs into it, killing by suffocation through lack of oxygen in the water.

The first method is suitable for killing the molluscs with tough shells, such as the Periwinkles, but is not recommended for most other species. In general, the second method is best, but the third method is preferable for the frail species and small species. For this task an old saucepan should be used, preferably with a lid to close it, as the aroma caused by the 'execution' of the living animals is not particularly fragrant. After they have been treated in this way the shells should be slowly and gently poured into a plastic colander, used for straining vegetables, to allow the water to drain away in the sink.

There are several methods of removing the dead mollusc from its shell. One of these is to bury shell and contents in sand or earth for several weeks until the body rots. A variation is to put the shell and mollusc into bowls of frequently-changed water until the mollusc's soft parts have rotted away. Or the shell and mollusc can be placed in or upon an ants' nest, the insects doing the job of body removal. But these methods have their snags. The collector who frequently obtained large numbers of living molluscs in their shells would equally require a lot of ants and ants' nests to work for him, and the high aroma of dead flesh from leaving them around in the garden is not exactly going to exhilarate the collector's neighbours! Shells buried in boxes of sand and earth would also have to be stacked somewhere, preferably out of sight, while the rotting process was taking place.

Preferably, as soon as they are cool enough to touch after 'execution' the shells should have their body contents removed. For the univalves a large pin or strong curved needle, firmly fixed into a wood holder as a handle, is a useful tool; bent wire will also serve; on the larger specimens a curved crochet hook can be used. Push these, or the pin or needle, into the thickest part of the mollusc that can be reached, then, pulling slowly and carefully, unwind the mollusc from within the shell's spiral.

These molluscs have a tendency to withdraw deeper into their shell or the flesh shrinks as the dead mollusc 'cooks', so be careful not to break them and leave the narrower hind portion inside. If you do, it may be possible to reach it with a pair of fine-pointed forceps. If not it may have to be rotted out of the shell. Sometimes it falls out if the shell is shaken with the aperture held downwards. The operculum should be carefully removed and dried. Next, rinse the interior of the shell by holding it, aperture upwards, under running water from a tap, shake the shell, then hold it aperture downwards to drain the water from it. If the exterior of an empty shell is dirty or discoloured with marine growth, such as algae this can be removed by washing the shell in a bowl of clean warm water containing a small amount of mild detergent, combined with the use of a reasonably soft brush. A nail brush can be gently used for larger shells, a toothbrush for smaller and frail specimens. For very small shells a child's stiff stencil or watercolour paint brush will be more practicable, and this brush is also useful for removing mud and growth from the ribs, ridges and suture. A wire brush must not be used on any shell as it scratches and damages the surface and would remove the outer coating or periostracum that should be carefully preserved. Do not use acid for cleaning shells. After washing, place the cleaned shells on blotting paper to dry, but not in direct hot sunshine as this will bleach them. The delicately patterned and colourful shells, such as Tellins, Sunset shells, etc., should be covered with paper when laid out to dry to shield them from hot sunlight for the same reason. When dry, push a small amount of cotton wool as a plug into the aperture of the univalve and on this put some adhesive. To the adhesive fix the operculum, ensuring that it is correct way up and looks as if it is in a natural position.

Bivalves are easier to deal with. If the mollusc is dead its adductor muscles relax and the hinge-ligament or muscle allows the valves to gape open. The soft body is then removed, using a sharp knife to cut through the adductor muscle attachments. The exterior and interior can then be washed as for univalves.

Until it is killed it is almost useless to attempt to open a bivalve. This usually means only that the knife blade damages the edges of the valves. After washing, cleaning and drying the bivalve close it in its natural position and keep it closed by placing an elastic band around it, or bind with fine soft thread. Do not use adhesive tape as this can mark or pull off the shell surface when removed later. The very small and fragile bivalves can be closed by putting them into a screw twist of tissue paper. If left like this until the hinge is completely dry, usually after about two to three weeks, when the elastic band or thread is taken off the bivalve should remain closed. A specimen of each bivalve with valves gaping apart should also be kept so that the interior, as well as the exterior, can be seen as part of a collection.

Lastly, the Limpets and limpet-shaped shell molluscs are treated in the same way, using a sharp knife to remove the contents, which usually come free without much difficulty.

The next step is to name each shell, but the value of a collection is considerably increased if more precise details are stated. This is the reason why such facts should be noted in the pocket notebook at the time of discovery. A small label can be laid alongside the shell in its container or glued on the side. Fix the label by each end but not in the middle, so that it can be easily removed if a different shell is later put in the compartment. Use Indian ink or waterproof ink and a fine-pointed pen to write the lettering. In addition to the English name add the scientific name, where found, tide state (low, half-tide, going out, etc.), the shore zone and type of habitat (on rocks, under seaweed or similar) or if dredged from deep water the type of sea bottom, if a living mollusc, newly-dead, or an old empty shell, also the date, time of day and your name. Labelling can also be taken further by adding brief details about the living mollusc, its colour, size, other marine creatures living with it and so on. Collectors can also give each shell a number, this being written in a separate logbook and alongside the same details are copied. This has the advantage that whereas only brief details can be put on a small label, in a logbook these can be expanded and much more useful information added, such as weather conditions, where exactly found on the habitat and anything of interest or unusual about the specimen.

Alternatively, some collectors prefer to use a card index system, with a separate card for each shell specimen. On this are added the same details with relevant number/numbers as for the previous method. These cards can be placed in alphabetical order, but is more preferable to arrange them in order of families, genera, species, classes and sub-classes. Every collector develops the system which he finds practicable and easiest for his quick reference.

How the collection is stored again depends on the circumstances of the collector. Glass-topped cabinets for mounted shells are dear to buy, although a collector may be fortunate to obtain one fairly cheaply by attending furniture auctions or finding one for sale in a second hand shop. Alternatively, a piece of furniture, such as an old-fashioned chest of drawers, or something similar, can be converted. An old wooden filing cabinet could probably be similarly adapted. It is advisable if possible to have drawers of different depths, so that the small shells can be accommodated in the shallow drawers and the larger shells in the deeper drawers. Each drawer should be divided into compartments, using plywood lengths notched to fit together. Incidentally, an oak cabinet, or oak drawers, should not be used if it can be avoided because oak, due to chemical action, causes a white crust that covers certain types of shell and destroys them.

The collector who is a competent carpenter can possibly adapt wooden boxes, fitting to each a glass or clear plastic sheet that slides in and out of one side on a runner as a lid. Similarly a shallow wood box can be made into a case to display small shells on a wall. Fix the shells to a sheet of stiff white card with adhesive, Canada balsam, on their underside, the label beneath each example, and pin the card to the box floor, over it fixing the glass or clear plastic sheet so that the specimens are visible. But do not hang the boxed display of shells where bright sunlight continually shines on them, or the colours of the shells will eventually fade.

If they lose their natural freshness, due to boiling and washing or age, shells should *not* be varnished, lacquered or shellacked. In time these may also discolour. A little mineral oil, rubbed carefully on the shell with a soft cloth, may restore some of the shell's brightness. A light household oil can also be used in this way to restore and preserve their glossy lustre but these oils should *not* be used on those shells that do not have the smooth glossy protective outer coat.

If the collection is to be housed in a spare room another method is to erect a wooden rack with several rows of shelves on which the cardboard boxes holding the shells can be placed. The cardboard boxes should also be divided into compartments using adhesive to fix the thick card lengths into position. Shells should not be just heaped into boxes or drawers, as the frequent sliding in and out or lifting of these will cause the brittle shells inside to knock against each other and become scratched, splintered and broken. All compartments in drawers and boxes should be lined either with foam rubber, cotton wool, felt, or other soft material to prevent damage to each shell. A miniature chest of drawers for small shells can be made by gluing together a stack of matchboxes and covering their exterior with white or coloured paper or adhesive plastic sheeting to improve their appearance. Each tray should also be lined. Similarly, the separate matchboxes can be kept inside one of the deeper drawers housing the remainder of the collection. Another way to keep small shells is inside glass tubes which originally contained chemists' tablets and pills, or bought from science equipment suppliers. A considerable number of tubes can be housed inside a cardboard box for security and safety. The label should be placed inside with the shell. If it is stuck securely on the tube outside a new one will have to be used to cover the old one every time a different type of shell is placed in the tube at a later date. The tubes should have a plug of cotton wool inside to prevent the shells sliding up and down the tube length and should be sealed with a cork.

Of course, collectors may have their own ideas how best to house their collection, to suit their especial purpose, and it will be satisfactory as long as it keeps the shells from being damaged while stored and free from dust and dirt, and prevents discolouration and fading.

2   The Mollusc and its Shell

To understand what a shell is, its purpose, and how it is created by a mollusc it is necessary to know some of a mollusc's anatomical details. The Mollusca, from the Latin 'molluscus', meaning soft, are a large group of unsegmented, invertebrate, soft-bodied animals, some of which are edible and popularly called 'shellfish'. Those concerned with this book have either a hard, single, external shell, the Univalves, or a shell comprising two valves, the Bivalves, but there are other molluscs which have a minute shell partly or entirely hidden in their body.

The univalves are members of the mollusc group called the Gastropods, meaning 'stomach-footed'. The shell is a single twisted spiral in shape, which varies considerably among the species, particularly in the number of whorls, or is conical, as in the Limpets, the shell being one large coil in which the earlier whorls have been amalgamated and disappeared.

The univalve mollusc has a broad, muscular, contractile 'foot' which partially protrudes from the shell 'aperture' and using this the mollusc can either progress over objects or burrow into a habitat. At the front of the upper 'foot' the mollusc has a distinct 'head', with two 'tentacles', the pair of 'eyes' being at the base of these 'tentacles'. The 'mouth' is in a lower central position, between the 'tentacles', on the underside of the 'head', inside which is the 'radula', a horny, ribbon-like 'tongue' having rows of 'teeth', which rasps the food into small particles that are passed along a tube into the 'stomach'. In the vegetarian Gastropods, feeding on seaweeds and other vegetation, the 'radula' is wide with rows of numerous small 'teeth'. The carnivorous Gastropods, feeding on living or dead flesh, have a narrow 'radula' and fewer but larger 'teeth'. In some examples of the latter the 'mouth' may be situated at the end of a long proboscis which can be used to penetrate a prey's shell so that the 'mouth' can obtain the victim's tissues inside it.

Sited on the upper hind end of the 'foot' there may also be an

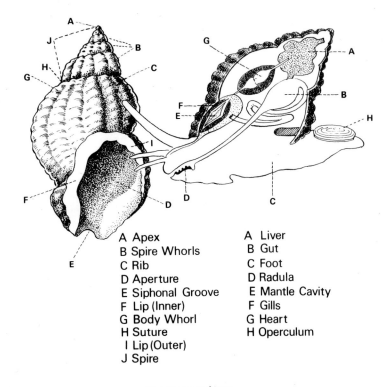

A Apex	A Liver
B Spire Whorls	B Gut
C Rib	C Foot
D Aperture	D Radula
E Siphonal Groove	E Mantle Cavity
F Lip (Inner)	F Gills
G Body Whorl	G Heart
H Suture	H Operculum
I Lip (Outer)	
J Spire	

Buccinum undatum

oval or circular horny or limy 'operculum', used as a protective cover or lid to close the 'aperture' when the mollusc has retreated into its shell as it is uncovered by the receding tide. Near the 'tentacles' on the 'head' there may also, depending on the species, be a 'siphon' tube, which draws in clean water which is internally passed over the 'gills' in the 'mantle cavity' to extract from the water oxygen needed for respiration. To accommodate the protruding 'siphon' the shell 'lip' has a groove or notch. The 'foot' continues as part of the soft body and combines with the lining membrane inside the shell called the 'mantle', one of the mollusc's most vital organs.

In sea water there is a large quantity of dissolved lime. This is extracted from the water and their food source by the univalve mollusc, the carbonate of lime, with animal-produced matter, being manufactured into conchiolin by the 'mantle' and then used to create the new layers of shell. Conchiolin is a semi-liquid material which rapidly hardens on exposure to water and air. Any area of the 'mantle' can manufacture and secrete the layers of conchiolin to repair accidental damage to and again make secure the shell, but only the 'mantle edge' is able to produce the colour or colours and patterning of the shell and where a repair is made this is a distinctive 'scar' because the original colour pattern is not reproduced.

As the univalve mollusc grows in size so the 'mantle' produces more conchiolin and the 'mantle edge' extends the shell size to allow for the mollusc's growth. This is done around the 'aperture', more being added on one side than the other, so the shell forms the spiral shape.

The shell is created in three layers. The first laid by the 'mantle' is the protecting outer or upper layer, which has all or some of the colour and patterning, and the 'periostracum'. This layer is backed by a second or central layer, which is crystalline and is itself supported by the third or inner layer which is thicker, smooth and polished, necessary to ensure that the shell does not irritate the mollusc's delicate tissues.

Thus this mode of life ensures that as the mollusc inside develops it does not have periodically to shed its hard covering shell, necessary to contain and protect its soft body, as is the case with some other forms of marine life. In some species even after the mollusc has matured and stopped growing the 'mantle edge' continues to produce conchiolin which results in a thick 'lip' being created on the edge of the 'aperture'. Those univalve shells, such as the Conches, which have large extensions on one side only and so appear lopsided, are created because one side of the mollusc's body is atrophied and has only a small area of 'mantle' tissue to produce conchiolin. The 'mantle edge' controls the final shape of all univalve shells. If the 'mantle edge' is flat, unwaved, then the shell will be smooth, but if the 'mantle edge' is irregular, waved and frilled, then the shell is ridged or spiked. But the shape of the univalve mollusc's shell also depends on the conditions of its habitat. Generally speaking, they are thick, tough, pointed and rounded, these molluscs occurring on rocky coasts, at middle shore zone, lower shore zone and below levels, where they need to have a shape which gives least resistance to the relentless pounding of the waves. Should it be dislodged by the waves the shell's shape allows it to be rolled along the shore without much harm.

There are exceptions, of course, and those species which live in less disturbed sandy or muddy habitats may be sculptured, with knobs and projections, while other species have different modifications, such as a long tapering shell or a flattened pyramid. Larger and thicker shells are usually created by molluscs in warmer climates than those in colder regions, due to the absorption and extraction of lime being higher in the former than in the latter. This is why some tropical species have massive thick shells.

The internal organs of the univalve mollusc also include a heart, kidney, liver, intestine, stomach, blood vessels, anus or vent, visceral ganglion, nerve cord, testes and sperm or oviduct. These vary in size and position depending on the different species' shell shape.

The Limpets (*Archaeogastropoda*), although univalves, differ in some respects from the coiled snail-like univalves. Their body contains the 'gills', 'respiratory cavity', 'foot', 'mantle', 'head', 'tentacles', 'mouth', 'radula', and other organs, these being accommodated inside the cone-shaped shell. Some species, *Patina*, have a ring of 'gills' around the 'foot', between the 'foot' and the 'mantle margin', while others, *Patella*, have a ring of 'gills' around the 'head' and 'foot'. The *Acmaea* have a single 'gill' near the head, while the *Diodora* have a pair of 'gills', the intaken water being expelled after use through a siphon in the single apical opening, the *Emarginula* expelling through a marginal slit.

The Limpet shell is really the last or 'body whorl', typical of snail-like univalves, which has been developed and enlarged to comprise the entire shell, while the other whorls are almost or entirely absent. The Limpet shell does not have a 'columella' to which the mollusc's body would be attached. Instead it has a large 'muscle' attaching it to the shell. The muscular 'foot' is broad and rounded, powerful and able to pull the shell downwards over and around the body and against the rock or object surface. This, allied with the conical shape of the broad-based shell which offers least resistance, enables the Limpet to survive strong currents and the pounding action of the sea. The more

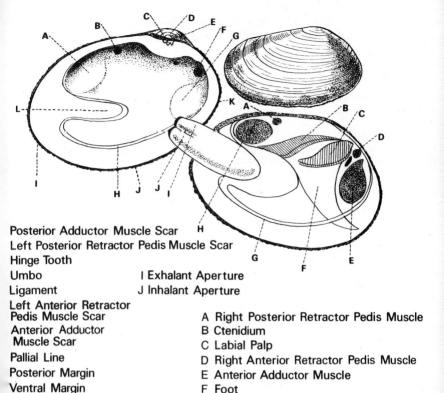

Posterior Adductor Muscle Scar
Left Posterior Retractor Pedis Muscle Scar
Hinge Tooth
Umbo   I Exhalant Aperture
Ligament   J Inhalant Aperture
Left Anterior Retractor
Pedis Muscle Scar
   Anterior Adductor   A Right Posterior Retractor Pedis Muscle
    Muscle Scar   B Ctenidium
Pallial Line   C Labial Palp
Posterior Margin   D Right Anterior Retractor Pedis Muscle
Ventral Margin   E Anterior Adductor Muscle
Anterior Margin   F Foot
Pallial Sinus   G Right Fold of Mantle
                            H Posterior Adductor Muscle

Lutraria lutraria

violent the waves the tighter the Limpet grips its site. Those
Limpet species with flattened cones have a tendency to occur in
the lower shore zone and below, whereas the Limpet species
with the pointed cones occur further up the rocky coast in the
middle shore zone and upper lower shore zone.

The bivalves are members of a mollusc group called the
Lamellibranchia or Pelecypoda, the latter meaning 'hatchet-
foot' and referring to the shape of the 'foot' in some species.

According to the type of habitat, they are separated into three
groups. One group contains the deep burrowers in mud and sand;
the second group occur on the surface, or only just beneath the

surface, of mud and sand, or attach themselves permanently or semi-permanently to rocks and objects; the third group are those which burrow at varying depths into clay, soft rock or chalk. The former two may have to be dug for to obtain good specimens when the empty shells are absent. The majority of bivalve molluscs live a sedentary or semi-sedentary existence after finding a suitable habitat at the start of their life. This is also the likely reason why bivalves tend to grow larger than univalves and huge specimens occur.

The shell is formed of two 'valves' between which their compressed body is enclosed for protection. The two 'valves' have a sometimes tough, internal or external, elastic-like 'ligament' uniting them. Here also is the 'hinge' of articulating 'teeth', taxodont or heterodont, which fit into grooves to secure the closed 'valves' from slipping, but some species do not have these 'teeth'. The 'valve margins' may also have interlocking 'crenations' for the same reason. One or two powerful 'adductor muscles' contract and serve to keep the 'valves' closed, but when these muscles are relaxed the 'ligament' separates or 'opens' the 'valves'. Close to the top edge of each 'valve' there is an 'umbo' or 'beak', which is the point of growth of the 'valves'. The 'valves' can be either equilateral or inequilateral, also equivalve or inequivalve.

The bivalve mollusc does not possess a 'head' or 'tentacles', like the univalves, but does have a 'mouth' without a 'radula'. The latter is not needed as the bivalves do not rasp their food into particles but take in a current of water through an 'inhalant siphon'. The plankton food particles suspended in the water are sieved from it by the very large 'gills' and passed to the 'mouth'. Near the 'mouth' there are two fleshy lobes or 'palps' on either side of it which select and control the flow of food to the 'mouth' so that it does not become choked. The unwanted water and particles are expelled through the 'exhalant siphon' above the 'inhalant siphon'. Both siphons are extensions of the 'mantle' and may be either a single fused unit (Razor, Gaper), or two separate tubes (Tellins). They can be extended to a considerable length by those species which are deep burrowers in the habitat and may be retractable within the 'valves' or permanently outside.

The bivalve mollusc respires at the same time by using the 'siphons'. Bivalves are either deposit feeders, obtaining their

Plate I **Cockles.** On the left examples of the **Common Edible Cockle** (*Cardium edule*), usual brown, also a grey variation. On the right, the **Rough Cockle** (*Cardium tuberculatum*)

Plate II **Gold-mouthed Turban** (*Turbo chrysostomus*) on the left; on the right the **Bleeding Tooth Nerite** (*Nerita peloronta*)

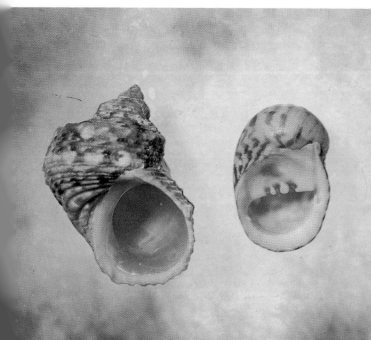

Plate III Interior of **Northern Green Abalone** (*Haliotis walallensis*)

Plate IV Exterior of **Northern Green Abalone** (*Haliotis walallensis*)

miscoscopic food particles lying as a sediment deposit on the surface of the habitat, or are suspension feeders, obtaining the food suspended in the water above the habitat.

The bivalve mollusc also has a usually-flattened 'foot', with muscles, which can be extended or withdrawn between the 'valves'. It is not used for crawling, like univalves, but for progression of a different kind, to burrow or dig rapidly into the habitat, or, as in the Piddocks, to grip the side of an excavated tunnel in soft rock when this is the habitat. In some species, such as the Mussels, the 'foot' also produces a liquid to create 'byssus' threads, by which the bivalve fixes its 'valves' to an object. The 'foot' is not present in all bivalves.

Like the univalves, the bivalve molluscs have a 'mantle' which produces the conchiolin to extend the shell 'valves' as the mollusc grows, but in the bivalve mollusc the 'mantle' is divided into two lobes, one per 'valve'. Some species, such as the Scallops, have 'eyes' on their 'mantle'.

The necessary internal organs of the bivalve mollusc also include a heart, kidney, liver, stomach, intestine, anus, digestive gland and reproductive system.

The bivalve mollusc's 'valves' on their interior, when empty, may bear the 'impressions' or 'scars' where the adductor muscles were attached. The 'pallial line' shows where the 'mantle' was attached and sited a distance inward from the shell's margin. This links the anterior (front) and posterior (hind) 'adductor muscle scars', which can be similar in size or one larger than the other (Mussels). In some bivalves (Scallops) the 'anterior muscle scar' is absent and only a central muscle 'scar' is present. When the 'siphons' are retractable in a species or protrude between the 'mantle' this may be evidence by a curve or u-shaped 'notch' in the 'pallial line', called the 'pallial sinus'.

Sometimes shell collectors have difficulty in deciding which is the 'right' and which is the 'left' valve of a bivalve shell. It is important to know this, because this can make the task much easier of identifying certain bivalves which have one 'valve' different to the other 'valve', particularly if these are found separated. If the bivalve is collected alive, or with the mollusc intact inside the 'valves' it should be remembered that the 'foot' is at the anterior or front end of the shell. The 'siphon' is positioned at the posterior or hind end of the shell. If the bivalve is placed with the 'hinge ligament' uppermost and the 'siphon' towards and the 'foot' away from the collector, the 'left valve' will be the 'valve' on their left-hand side and the 'right valve' on their right-hand side. Similarly, when the empty shell has both 'valves' if it is placed with the 'beaks' uppermost and the 'hinge ligament' between the collector and the 'beaks', the 'beaks' or 'umbones' will usually be turned forward away from the collector, and the 'left valve' will be on the left-hand side and the 'right valve' on the right-hand side. As another guide, the 'pallial sinus' is also positioned at the posterior or hind end of the 'valve'.

3   Bivalves

EDIBLE OYSTERS

Little needs to be said about the Edible Oysters, which, dating back before the period of the Roman Empire, have been eaten as a health-giving food for centuries. The shells can vary considerably in shape. Occasionally pearls are produced, but these are not nacreous and have no commercial value.

American Blue Point Oyster, Eastern Oyster (*Crassostrea virginica*):
East coast U.S.A., Gulf of Mexico. Not native to the British Isles. First introduced to Britain in the 1880's to 'plant' in oyster beds to supplement dwindling stocks of cultivated Edible Native or English Oysters, but has not established itself and rarely breeds, due to low temperature of British coastal waters.
Occurs below lower shore in clean, shallow water, attached to rocks, stones, shells, or lying unattached on clean sand. Rarely uncovered by sea at low tide while alive; empty shells cast up on higher shore levels.
Shell valves thick and elongated, more narrow-oval than round, with long, curved beaks, pointed towards the apex; inequivalve; upper valve smaller, cemented with the left or lower valve undermost. The lower or left valve is also deep, giving it a scoop-like resemblance. Exterior of valves uneven, with irregular growth lines.
Exterior shell colour, greyish-white; interior, pearly-white with purplish edging and muscle scars, often dark purple.
Measures up to 7 inches from beak to margin.

Edible, Flat, Native English or European Oyster (*Ostrea edulis*):
South-west and south-east coast England, especially Thames

estuary, also European coasts, particularly west coast France. Common, although now extinct in some habitats where formerly common, due to pollution, severe winters, over-fishing or destruction by predators. To counter this the Portuguese Oyster (*C. angulata*) and American Oyster (*C. virginica*) have periodically been introduced to supplement the native stock. But for this oysters would have disappeared long ago from British coasts. The oyster occurs in dense numbers beyond lower shore in shallow water of estuaries and bays, but in deep water occurs singly, some of the latter examples often reaching a larger size. Uses a cement to attach itself to rocks, stones and other objects, by its left or lower valve, although it may become detached and be found lying on the habitat bed. The single, empty, valves are cast up on the lower shore, often encrusted with acorn barnacles, marine worm tubes or with small holes bored by a yellow sponge, *Cliona celata*.

The inequivalve shell valves are rounded, thick and flat, with irregular edges, but no hinge teeth, the exterior being rough. The upper or right valve is plain, flat or slightly concave; the under, lower or left valve is larger, convex and has overlapping, irregular growth layers.

Exterior shell colour, brownish-white or dirty greyish; interior, smooth, whitish and pearl-like, the muscle scar being white.

Measures up to 4 inches in diameter in cultivation beds; deep water specimens may be 6 inches or larger.

Native Pacific Oyster (*Ostrea lurida*):
Alaska; Pacific coast Canada and U.S.A. to lower California.
Occurs on lower shore and below.
Shell narrow-elongated, curved at umbones; exterior rough with coarse growth lines.
Exterior shell colour, brownish, greyish-white; interior, olive-green.
Measures up to 2 inches in length.

Portuguese Oyster (*Crassostrea angulata*):
South-west and south-east coast England, especially Thames estuary, also European coastline, particularly south-west France. Occurs in same habitats as Native English or European Oyster (*O. edulis*). It has been imported into Britain for 'planting' in

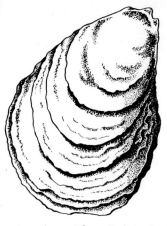

American Blue Point Oyster, Eastern Oyster (*Crassostrea virginica*)

Edible, Flat, Native English or European Oyster (*Ostrea edulis*)

Native Pacific Oyster (*Ostrea lurida*)

Portuguese Oyster (*Crassostrea angulata*)

beds to supplement native stocks. Does occasionally spawn in south-east British habitats. Occurs in shallow water of estuaries, bays and creeks. Single empty valves are washed ashore, often encrusted with tubes of marine worms, acorn barnacles and other marine growths.

The thick irregular valves are narrow-elongated, with concentric ridges and some radiating ribs and appearing somewhat distorted. It is identified from the American Blue Point Oyster (*O. Virginica*) by having a strongly-crenulated or fluted margin, whereas *C. virginica* has only a slightly wavy, almost smooth, margin. The valves are inequivalve; the smaller upper or right valve is flat, the larger left or lower valve being deep and scoop-like. Exterior shell colour, dirty-white, cream or pale brown with purple blotches and a brown periostracum; interior, pearly-white with purple muscle scar.

Measures up to 7 inches from hinge to margin.

PEARL OYSTERS

There are several oysters which produce pearls. They are allied to the Wing Oysters, but only distantly related to the edible oysters. Pearls are formed by layers of calcium carbonate laid around an irritant – a grain of sand or something similar – which has reached the mantle. Often, however, the nacre or mother-of-pearl forms irregular layers to overcome the irritant. Even when pearl shaped they may be too small to have a commercial value. Pearl oysters occur in warm tropical waters.

Atlantic Pearl Oyster (*Pinctada radiata*):
South-east coast U.S.A., Gulf of Mexico, Brazil.
Occurs below lower shore, on rocks.
Shell thin, flattened, brittle, with a short posterior 'wing' and sometimes long spines on the periostracum.
Exterior shell colour, variable, pale to mid-brown, interior, pearly.
Measures up to 3 inches in width.

Black-Lip Pearl Oyster (*Pinctada margaritifera*):
South-east Asia, Persian Gulf, Gulf of Bahrein, Kuwait, Red Sea, Sudan, deep water, on rocks.
Shell rounded, with crenellations on margin; a straight dorsal hinge. It secretes the nacre that forms the world's finest pearls, but the black 'lip' or rim of the valves has practically no commercial value.
Measures 6 inches in width.

Ceylon Pearl Oyster (*Pinctada vulgaris*):
West coast Ceylon, Indonesia, New Guinea, Philippines.
Occurs in deep water on sand.
It forms its pearls by using the nacre to overcome irritation by a

tapeworm, parasitic on the rays, which lives part of its life cycle within this oyster shell, the rays being infected by eating the oyster.

Golden-Lip or Pearl Button Oyster (*Pinctada maxima*):
Persian Gulf, Red Sea, Sudan coast.
Occurs in deep water.
The nacre it secretes in forming pearls is of lesser quality, but, as its name indicates, the silvery-gold 'lip' or rim was in demand commercially to manufacture mother-of-pearl buttons until these were made cheaply artificially from plastics.

Japanese Pearl Oyster (*Pinctada mertensi*):
Japan.
Occurs in deep water, on rocky bottoms.
Shell rounded, irregular with crenulations; has straight hinge.
Produces fine quality pale pink, white and yellowish pearls.
Exterior shell colour, pale and dark brown, interior, pearly.
Measures up to 3 inches in width.

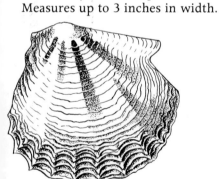
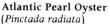

Atlantic Pearl Oyster
(*Pinctada radiata*)

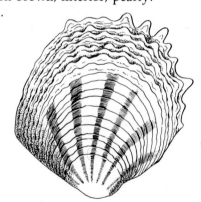

Golden-Lip or Pearl Button Oyster
(*Pinctada maxima*)

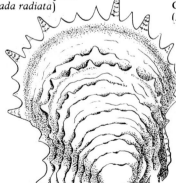

Japanese Pearl Oyster
(*Pinctada mertensi*)

THORNY OYSTERS

The Thorny Oysters are related to the Scallops, to which the valves have a resemblance, except that they bear long spines. The latter may become very lengthy if the habitat is calm water. They have eyes on the edge of the mantle. Tropical specimens are varied in colour and pattern and are sometimes called Chrysanthemum shells. They are not related to the true oysters.

Atlantic Thorny Oyster (*Spondylus americanus*):
South-east coast U.S.A., Caribbean.
Occurs below lower shore, attached to rocks and may have covering of seaweeds, sponges and other growths.
Shell thick and scallop-shaped, with 'ears' on either side of ball-socket hinge. Spines up to 3 inches in length.
Exterior shell colour, variable, white, yellowish-white, bright red, purple, with yellow spines; interior, white with yellow margin.
Measures up to 6 inches in diameter.

Pacific Thorny Oyster (*Spondylus princeps*):
Gulf of California, west coast Mexico, Central America to Panama.
Occurs below lower shore, in deep water, attached by a byssus to rocks, stones and other objects. Often encrusted with marine growths.
Shell thick, almost round, scallop-shape, with 'ears' on either side of the ball-and-socket hinge. Spines and projections up to $1\frac{1}{2}$ inches in length.
Exterior shell colour, purplish-red, spines sometimes being darker; interior, white with purplish-red margin.
Measures up to 6 inches in diameter.

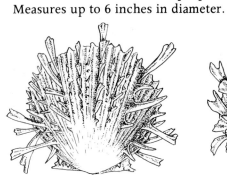

Atlantic Thorny Oyster
(*Spondylus americanus*)

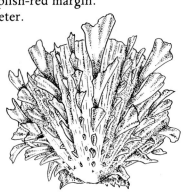

Pacific Thorny Oyster
(*Spondylus princeps*)

WING OYSTERS

The Wing Oysters are distantly related to the true Edible Oysters and are edible. Occasionally they produce pearls but these are not usually commercially valuable.

Atlantic Wing Oyster (*Pteria colymbus*):
East and south-east coast U.S.A., West Indies, Brazil.
Occurs below lower shore, in shallow water and deep water, attached to objects; empty valves cast ashore.
So-named because of its shape which makes it unmistakable; the inequilateral valves have wing-like processes on the posterior side of the beak or umbo, which is sited far forward. In front of the umbo there is a rounded triangular-shaped anterior 'ear' with a byssal notch beneath it, through which a byssus protrudes to attach the shell to the object.
Exterior shell colour, dark and light brown; interior, iridescent pearly blue, but margin is not pearly.
Measures up to $2\frac{1}{2}$ inches in width.

Western Wing Oyster (*Pteria sterna*):
South-west Pacific coast U.S.A., Mexico, Central America, Panama.
Occurs on lower shore and below, on sandy mud.
Shell shape similar to Atlantic Wing Oyster, but posterior wing longer.
Exterior shell colour, purplish-brown with paler rays; interior, pearly.
Measures up to 3 inches in width.

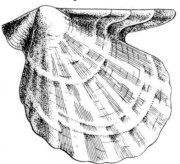

Atlantic Wing Oyster
(*Pteria colymbus*)

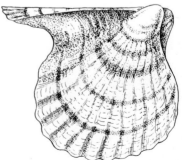

Western Wing Oyster
(*Pteria sterna*)

41

Wing Oyster, Wing-Shell (*Pteria hirundo*):
South-west coast England, but here rare; Bay of Biscay; Mediterranean coasts.
Occurs below lower shore on muddy sand; empty valves cast ashore.
Shell similar in shape to Atlantic Wing Oyster with long posterior wing swept more horizontally backwards.
Exterior shell colour, yellowish or muddy-brown, sometimes with purplish streaks; interior, pearly white.
Measures up to 3 inches in width.

SADDLE OYSTERS, JINGLE SHELLS

It used to be thought, mistakenly, that the Saddle Oysters were young examples of the true oysters or smaller relatives of the true Edible Oysters. Neither is the case; the Saddle Oysters are related to the mussels. The chief difference in the Saddle Oysters is that the flat, thin, lower or under-valve has an oval or pear-shaped hole near the hinge and through this a byssus 'plug' is projected to attach the bivalve mollusc to a rock, stone, empty shell or other object, unlike the hole-less Edible Oyster which uses a cement. Here the Saddle Oysters stay for their life unless removed by a predator or accident. As the valves develop their margins conform to the alignment of the object to which the bivalve is attached.

Common Jingle Shell, Atlantic Jingle (*Anomia simplex*):
East coast U.S.A., Caribbean.
Occurs on lower shore and below, in warm coastal water, attached to rocks, stones, other objects; empty valves washed ashore.
Shell circular, thin, inequivalve; lower valve smaller and flatter than deeply hollow, convex upper valve.
Exterior shell colour, yellowish-orange or silvery-grey; interior, pearly-white.
Measures up to 2 inches in diameter.

Heteranomia Squamula:
British Isles, west coast Europe, from Scandinavia to France.

Occurs below lower shore, attached to stones, empty shells, sea-weed, even the carapace of a lobster or crab.

Shell almost round; the flat, thin, lower valve has a pear-shaped opening from which extrudes a plug used to fix it to an object; has no hinge teeth; two muscle scars are 'stepped', but not radially striated (see Ribbed Saddle Oyster and Saddle Oyster). Exterior shell colour, dull white.

Measures up to $\frac{1}{2}$ inch in diameter; the smallest of the Saddle Oysters.

Ribbed Saddle Oyster (*Monia patelliformis*):
British Isles.

Occurs below lower shore, in deeper water, attached to rocks, stones, shells, other objects, in the same manner as the Saddle Oyster; empty valves may be cast on the middle and lower shore. Shell is almost round, much flatter, and has up to 30 wavy ribs radiating from the beak or umbo near the margin; it may also have a number of fine, crowded, overlapping scales. The upper valve has two separated muscle scars.

Exterior shell colour, greyish- or greenish-white with red-brown streaks and spots; interior, glossy white.

Measures up to an inch in diameter.

Heteranomia Squamula

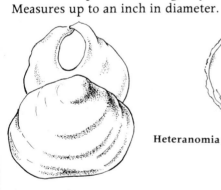

Common Jingle Shell, Atlantic Jingle (*Anomia simplex*)

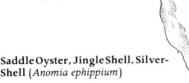

Saddle Oyster, Jingle Shell, Silver-Shell (*Anomia ephippium*)

43

Saddle Oyster, Jingle Shell, Silver-Shell (*Anomia ephippium*):
British Isles.
Occurs on the middle and lower shore, attached to rocks, stones, empty shells, a dead crab's carapace and other objects.
Shell is almost round; lower valve flat, upper valve convex; thin, with umbo near the margin; the upper valve interior has also three adductor muscle scars.
Exterior shell colour, dull white, with yellow, pinkish, or brown; interior, glossy silver-white.
Measures up to $2\frac{1}{2}$ inches in diameter.

SCALLOPS OR PECTENS

These hinged, rounded equivalve shells, except the inequivalve Great or Edible Scallop, are considered by some conchologists to be the most beautiful and attractive of the bivalves, because of their shape, patterning and, in some examples, delicate colouration, these factors making immediate family recognition possible. An elastic-like ligament extends along the variably-shaped, familiar 'ears' or 'wings', on each side of the beak or umbo, to connect the two valves. The scallop has one fused adductor muscle placed centrally. Single empty valves are washed ashore after storms and rough seas. Scallops species that are not sedentary can swim vigorously through the water by rapidly opening and closing their valves, and by using the edge of their mantle can steer in the direction they want to go. The edges of this mantle also have tentacles and up to a hundred eyes. Several species are commercially fished, for the single muscle, on the U.S.A. coast.

Atlantic Bay Scallop (*Aequipecten irradians*):
East coast Canada and U.S.A.
Occurs below lower shore, among eel-grass.
Shell rounded, with up to 18 low, rounded ribs; more flat, less convex.
Exterior shell colour, greyish or pale brown.
Measures up to 3 inches in diameter.

Calico Scallop (*Aequipecten gibbus*):
South-east coast U.S.A., Caribbean, Gulf of Mexico, to Brazil.
Occurs on lower shore and below.
Shell rounded, has up to 21 squarish ribs.
Exterior shell colour, variable, white with purplish-brown wavy markings or mottling, yellow with dark brown wavy markings or mottling, pale lilac with darker brownish markings, creamy with orange wavy markings or mottling. The patterning may be extensive or consist of a few wavy streaks or flecks.
Measures up to 2 inches in diameter.

Giant Pacific Scallop (*Pecten caurinus*):
Alaska, Pacific coast Canada and U.S.A.
Occurs in deep water.
Shell rounded, with up to 17 flattened, rounded ribs; upper valve nearly flat with narrow ribs, lower valve semi-convex with wider ribs; one wing or ear is reduced, the other ear or wing being noticeably larger.
Exterior shell colour, upper valve brownish-red with mauve on the wings and valve margin, lower valve, yellowish-brown with a brown-red margin.
Measures up to 8 inches in diameter.

Giant Rock Scallop (*Hinnites multirugosus*):
Alaska, Pacific coast Canada and U.S.A.
Occurs on lower shore and below, attached by lower valve to rocks, wharf and pier piles, etc.
Shell more oyster-shaped than circular, with irregular ears; exterior of shell has up to 18 ribs, each with short spiny projections and narrower, finer ribs in between.
Exterior shell colour, red-brown; interior, white, but has a purplish blotch along interior hinge line.
Measures up to 8 inches in diameter.

Great Scallop, Edible Scallop or Clam (*Pecten maximus*):
British Isles.
Occurs on the lower shore and in deep water, on sand. It is commercially fished on the south-east and east coasts. A trawl is used as its rapid mobility allows it to escape an oncoming dredge easily.

45

Shell rigid, inequivalve, nearly round; the smaller upper or left valve is almost flat, the lower, right or under valve is convex; has up to 15 widely spaced, broad, round-topped, several ridged ribs.

Exterior shell colour, plain yellowish-white, brown, reddish-brown or grey; interior, glossy white with dark brown or purple-brown margin.

Measures up to 5 inches in diameter; largest British scallop.

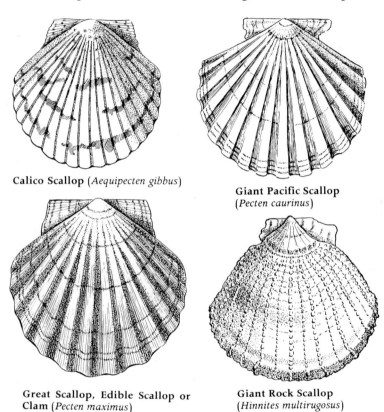

Calico Scallop (*Aequipecten gibbus*)

Giant Pacific Scallop
(*Pecten caurinus*)

Great Scallop, Edible Scallop or
Clam (*Pecten maximus*)

Giant Rock Scallop
(*Hinnites multirugosus*)

Hunchback Scallop (*Chlamys distorta*):
British Isles.

Occurs on the lower shore and in deep water, especially rocky coasts, in rock crevices, in empty shells or may be on oarweed holdfasts. It attaches its right or lower valve permanently to this with a cement.

Shell approximately rounded, is irregular and distorted, compressed or twisted, because of confined growth in the crevices that it fits into, causing its hunchbacked appearance. It has up to 70 narrow, sharp, prickly, alternately large and small, ribs.

Exterior shell colour, white, yellowish, brown, red, slate-grey, with similar coloured streaks or blotches.

Measures up to $1\frac{1}{2}$ inches in diameter.

Kelp-Weed Scallop (*Leptopecten latiauratus*):
Pacific coast California, U.S.A.

Occurs on lower shore, in shallow water, on kelp-weed and stones.

Shell rounded, thin, with up to 16 low, squarish ribs.

Exterior shell colour, pale brown, yellowish-brown, red-brown, with white irregular wavy patterning.

Measures up to an inch in diameter.

Lion's-Paw Scallop (*Lyropecten nodosus*):
South-east coast U.S.A., Caribbean, Brazil.

Occurs below lower shore, in deep water.

Shell rounded, with up to 9 prominent ribs bearing large hollow protuberances or nodes and smaller riblets, giving the resemblance of a lion's paw; margin of valves wavy.

Exterior shell colour, reddish-purple, brownish, orange or yellow, with darker banding.

Measures up to 4 inches in diameter.

Mediterranean Scallop, Jacob's Scallop (*Pecten jacobaeus*):
Mediterranean.

Occurs below lower shore.

Shell shape similar to Great Scallop, but has angular ribs instead of rounded-top ribs. This scallop was the original used for pilgrims' badges and heraldic coats-of-arms.

Exterior shell colour, pale whitish-pink or lilac, with white ribs.

Measures up to 5 inches in diameter.

Queen or Quin Scallop (*Chlamys opercularis*):
British Isles.

Occurs sometimes on lower shore, but usually in deeper water,

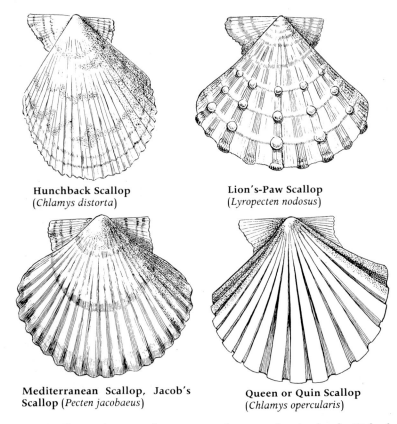

Hunchback Scallop
(*Chlamys distorta*)

Lion's-Paw Scallop
(*Lyropecten nodosus*)

Mediterranean Scallop, Jacob's Scallop (*Pecten jacobaeus*)

Queen or Quin Scallop
(*Chlamys opercularis*)

especially on clean sandy coasts; swims together in shoals. Fished for commercially.

Shell rounded, with up to 20 broad, round-topped ribs; the ears or wings are nearly equal.

Exterior shell colour, very variable, white, yellow, orange, reds, purples, browns, may be streaked, blotched and spotted. A beautiful specimen is the pale pink with rose-red patterning. Measures up to 3 inches in diameter.

San Diego Scallop (*Pecten diegensis*):
South-west Pacific coast U.S.A.
Occurs below lower shore, in deep water.
Shell rounded, with up to 24 prominent, flattened, grooved ribs, those on the flatter upper valve being narrower, more rounded

Plate V Three views of the **Sundial Shell** or **Staircase Shell** (*Architectonica perspectiva*)

Plate VI Upper surface view of **Tiger Cowrie** (*Cypraea tigris*)

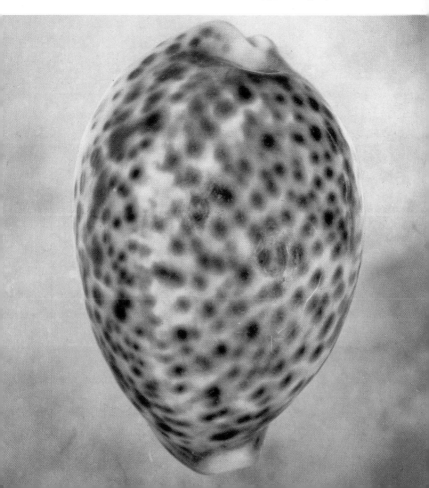

Plate VII Two views of the **Pelican's Foot Shell** (*Aporrhais pes-pelecani*)

Plate VIII Two views of the **Radix Murex** (*Murex radix*)

and wider spaced; shell margin crenulated.
Exterior shell colour, brownish-red; interior, white, with brownish-red margin and wings.
Measures up to 4 inches in diameter.

Seven-Rayed Scallop (*Chlamys septemradiata*):
British Isles, chiefly Scotland, northern England, western Europe.
Occurs below lower shore, on rough bottoms, in deep water.
Quickly recognised by the 7 narrow, rounded-top ribs, the central one being the largest, widely spaced apart, with rounded valleys between ribs in the thin brittle shell. Despite name 10 ribs may be present or less than 7, but this is usual number.
Exterior shell colour, brown-red, though it may have white flecks, or may be entirely white.
Measures up to $1\frac{3}{4}$ inches in diameter.

Tiger Scallop (*Chlamys tigerina*):
British Isles.
Occurs occasionally on the lower shore, but usually in deep water, on rocky stony bottoms.
Shell rounded with unequal-sized ears or wings, up to 30 fine radiating ribs, up to 10 of these being broad and distinct.
Exterior shell colour, very variable, purple, brown, yellow, sometimes pure white, with spots, stripes, or bands, suggesting its name.
Measures up to $1\frac{1}{4}$ inches in diameter.

Variegated Scallop (*Chlamys varia*):
British Isles.
Occurs on the lower shore and in deep water.
Shell valves tend more to oval than round, the ears or wings being unequal, there also being up to 30 equal-sized ribs with blunt 'prickles' on their surface.
Exterior shell colour, very variable, sometimes one colour, yellow, red, pink, brown, purple, rarely white, or mottled and streaked with several colours.
Measures up to $1\frac{1}{2}$ inches in diameter.

Seven-Rayed Scallop
(*Chlamys septemradiata*)

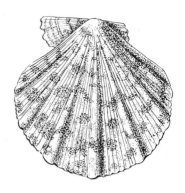

Tiger Scallop (*Chlamys tigerina*)

Variegated Scallop (*Chlamys varia*)

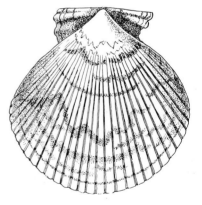

Zig-Zag Scallop (*Pecten ziczac*)

Zig-Zag Scallop (*Pecten ziczac*):
South-east coast U.S.A., Caribbean.
Occurs below lower shore.
Shell circular, with up to 40 ribs on the upper valve and up to
20 broad, wide spaced ribs on the lower valve.
Exterior shell colour, pale brown and reddish-brown, some zig-
zag darker markings: interior, upper valve, white.
Measures up to 3 inches in diameter.

FILE SHELLS, LIMA SHELLS (U.S.A.)

Named because of their rasp-like covering. Each adult creates a protective 'nest', by using byssus threads and mucus to fix together debris, stones, shell fragments, seaweed, which is attached to oarweeds' holdfasts or similar large seaweeds. Empty valves are occasionally cast ashore.

Fragile File Shell (*Lima loscombi*):
British Isles.
Occurs below lower shore, on mud and gravel bottoms.
Shell similar to L. hians, but more convex, with up to 60 sharp ribs. Shells thinner, gape only slightly on dorsal side; inequivalve; has orange tentacles as L. hians.
Exterior shell colour, white.
Measures up to $\frac{3}{4}$ inch in length.

Gaping File Shell (*Lima hians*):
Northern British Isles, Anglesey, Isle of Man.
Occurs below lower shore, on stony gravel bottoms.
Shell, broad oval or rhomboidal in shape twisted to one side; equivalve; up to 60 ribs radiate from the beak. Even when closed valves have wide gape. Living example immediately identified by extremely long unwithdrawable orange-red sensory tentacles.
Exterior shell colour, white, though it tends to brown or discolour with age.
Measures up to $1\frac{1}{4}$ inches in length.

Lima Glaciata:
South coast British Isles, Channel Isles.
Occurs below lower shore.
A variety of L. hians, but narrower, with up to 40 ribs.
Exterior shell colour, white.
Measures up to $\frac{1}{2}$-inch in length.

Rough Lima, Rough File Clam (*Lima scabra*):
South-east coast U.S.A., Caribbean, West Indies.
Occurs on lower shore.
Shell broad-oval, with two ears similar sized; coarse sculpturing of the numerous irregular ribs; wide gape. Living examples have

51

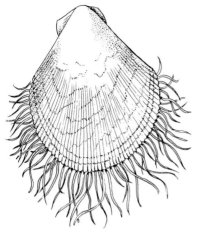

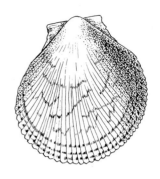

Rough Lima, Rough File Clam (*Lima scabra*)

Fragile File Shell (*Lima loscombi*)

long scarlet tentacles.
Exterior shell colour, brownish; interior, white.
Measures up to 4 inches in diameter.

Spiny Lima (*Lima lima*):
South-east coast U.S.A., Caribbean.
Occurs on lower shore, under rocks and stones.
Shell similar to Rough Lima, with numerous sharp-spined radial ribs, but anterior ear larger than posterior ear; narrow gape.
Exterior shell colour, whitish-brown; interior, white.
Measures up to 2 inches in diameter.

PINNA OR FAN MUSSELS (British Isles): PEN SHELLS OR SEA PENS (U.S.A.)

Although so-called, these molluscs are not related to the true Edible Mussel species, but closer to the Wing Oysters. They are, however, occasionally fished for food. When hunting for Pinna shoes or strong-soled sandals must be worn. The curved posterior margins of the valves project slightly above the surface of the habitat and, being razor-like, could inflict serious injuries to the soles of the feet of any collector who treads heavily on them barefooted.

Amber Pen Shell (*Pinna carnea*):
East coast U.S.A., Caribbean.
Occurs below lower shore, in coral sand, or may be attached by byssus threads to immersed rocks and stones.
Thin brittle shell, wedge-shaped or like a half-closed fan with posterior end curved; up to 10 radial spiny or smooth ridges, the umbo or beak is forward at narrow anterior end, in front of which the valve margin forms a point.
Exterior shell colour, amber, pale orange.
Measures up to 6 inches in length.

Fan Mussel (*Pinna fragilis*):
British Isles.
Occurs on sheltered lower shore and below, where it can be found buried with the umbonal or pointed end downwards in muddy sand or gravel or attached to buried rocks or stones by a byssus.
Thin, frail, easily broken shell shaped like a half-closed fan with knife-edge, gaping, posterior end curved; the umbo or beak is forward at the narrow anterior end, in front of which the valve margin forms a blunt point.
Exterior shell colour, glossy brown-yellow.
Measures up to 15 inches in length and 6 to 8 inches broad at posterior end; the largest British bivalve.

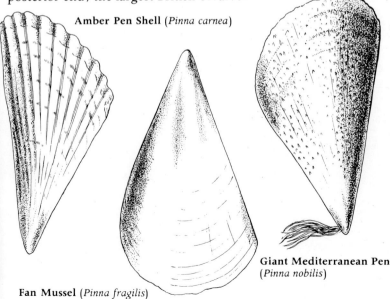

Amber Pen Shell (*Pinna carnea*)

Giant Mediterranean Pen (*Pinna nobilis*)

Fan Mussel (*Pinna fragilis*)

Giant Mediterranean Pen (*Pinna nobilis*):
Mediterranean coasts.
Occurs below lower shore, in soft sand.
Shell similar in shape to Fan Mussel. The long silky byssal threads used to be collected and woven into a highly-prized cloth.
Exterior shell colour, golden yellow-brown.
Measures up to 14 inches in length.

MUSSELS

Their hinged shell is equivalve, approximately pear-shaped, with an umbo on the upper surface or at the narrow end of the valve. The reason for the streamlined valves is that their shape gives least resistance to wave action. Mussels attach themselves by strong byssus to rocks, stones, pier piles and other objects, sometimes creating large 'beds' or colonies. These byssus threads are placed in varying directions so that the mussel swings to face the approaching flow of tide water with its narrow beak end, the posterior end acting as a vane. This reduces the risk of its being dislodged by forceful water. Certain mussel species are pests in oyster beds because their numerous byssus causes mud deposition that, added to the weight of mussel numbers, smothers the oysters. The interior of most species' valves are glossy and iridescent.

Common Edible Mussel (British Isles), Blue Mussel (U.S.A.) (*Mytilus edulis*)

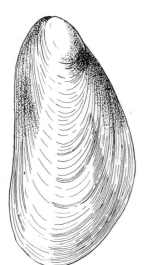

Bean Horse Mussel (*Modiolus phaseolinus*)

Horse Mussel (British Isles), Northern Horse Mussel (U.S.A.) (*Modiolus modiolus*)

Hooked Mussel (*Brachidontes recurvus*)

Bean Horse Mussel (*Modiolus phaseolinus*):
British Isles.
Occurs on the lower shore and below, attached to rocks, stones. Shell beak is blunt-pointed, with the umbo on the upper surface. The thick yellow-brown periostracum is split up to form 'thorns' over the posterior half of shell surface. If these are removed shell is bean-shaped. Hinge has rounded teeth. Byssus may have shell fragments adhering to them
Exterior shell colour, under periostracum, yellowish-purple.
Measures up to $\frac{3}{4}$-inch in length.

Bearded Horse Mussel (*Modiolus barbatus*):
South and west coast England and Wales, south and west Ireland. Occurs on the lower shore and below, on rocky, stony bottoms. Shell beak blunt-pointed with umbo on upper surface. The thick yellow-brown periostracum is split up to form prolonged 'thorns', over the posterior half of the shell surface, which is serrated or barbed on one side only.
Exterior shell colour, under periostracum, yellow or scarlet-red.
Measures up to 2 inches in length.

Common Edible Mussel (British Isles), Blue Mussel (U.S.A.) (*Mytilus edulis*):
British Isles, west coast Europe, east and Pacific coast U.S.A. Occurs on the middle shore and lower shore, attached in large numbers to rocks, stones, pier piles, jetties, breakwaters, wrecks, buoys and submerged objects, but exposed at low tide. Empty valves common in these habitats. Gathered from 'beds' for human food, but sometimes become poisonous with a toxic substance and so cause serious and sometimes fatal illness; also used for fish bait; the crushed shell has commercial uses.
Variable in size, shape and colour, but easily recognised. Generally, beak blunt-pointed with umbo at valve tip.
Exterior shell colour, dark blue, almost blackish-blue, sometimes greenish, with paler areas towards umbo; interior, glossy, paler blue or pearly white.
Measures up to 4 inches in length.
There are two varieties. The first, *var.* pellucida, has brown or purple ray markings on its thin, glossy valves. The second, *var.* pallida, is a yellowish-straw colour.

Hooked Mussel (*Brachidontes recurvus*):
East coast U.S.A., Caribbean.
Occurs on lower shore, on pier piles and similar.
Shell flat, broad, with a sharply curved beak and umbo, from which numerous curved ridges radiate to the margin.
Exterior shell colour, greenish-grey, brownish-grey; interior, reddish-brown with a white margin.
Measures up to an inch in length.

Horse Mussel (British Isles), Northern Horse Mussel (U.S.A.) (*Modiolus modiolus*):
British Isles, Isle of Man, north-east coast, U.S.A.
Occurs in deep water offshore, attached to rocks on muddy bottoms; occasionally carried ashore attached to large seaweeds, or as empty valves after rough seas. Young examples may occur in rock pools on the lower shore.
Shell thick, blunt-pointed, with bulging beak or umbo on its upper surface; coarse growth lines; thick periostracum forms long horny fringe processes with plain edges in young, which may bear coating of other shell and stone fragments. These fibres wear off with age.
Exterior shell colour, dark purplish-brown or blackish-brown with paler area on and near umbo; interior, pearly-white.
Measures up to 6 inches in length; the largest British mussel.

Mediterranean Mussel (*Mytilus galloprovincialis*):
South-west coast England, south Wales, Orkney.
Occurs on middle shore and lower shore, attached to rocks, stones, pier piles, wrecks and submerged objects.
Similar to *M. edulis* except shell is less angular on upper margin, the umbones being more pointed and are down-curving; fringe of tissues on mantle-edge is dark blue, purple, near-black in this species, but white or straw-coloured in *M. edulis*.
Exterior shell colour, dark blue, almost blackish-blue; interior, glossy paler blue or pearly whitish-blue.
Measures up to 5 inches in length.

Tulip Mussel (*Modiolus americanus*):
East coast U.S.A., Caribbean.
Occurs on lower shore and below, attached to rocks, stones, shell

fragments and similar.

Shell thin, blunt-pointed; smooth; growth lines less prominent; periostracum sometimes hairy.

Exterior shell colour, pale brown and may have mauve or pink rays; periostracum brown; interior, whitish, with pale brown, rose-pink, mauve-blue, yellow.

Measures up to 2 inches in length.

ARK SHELLS

The Ark Shells occur in both tropical warm and cool waters. They usually have a squarish shape, a horny ligament, a straight hinge and numerous taxodont teeth. Some species are attached to rocks and objects by a byssus, others burying in a muddy sand habitat. They are edible and gathered commercially in certain parts of the world.

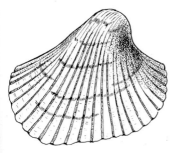

Blood Ark (*Anadara ovalis*)

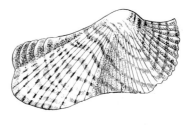

Noah's Ark, Zebra Ark, Turkey Wing (*Arca zebra*)

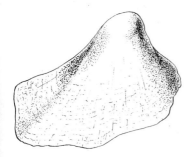

Noah's Ark (*Arca tetragona*)

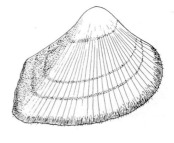

Milky Ark (*Arca lactea*)

Blood Ark (*Anadara ovalis*):
East and south-east coast U.S.A., Caribbean.
Occurs on lower shore and below, on sandy bottoms.
Shell thick, cockle-shaped, almost round, with curved umbones close to the hinge and up to 35 prominent smooth ribs, separated by narrow grooves, radiating from umbones to shell margin. So-named because it is one of the few molluscs having red blood. Exterior shell colour, dark brownish with paler area on umbones; interior, white.
Measures up to 2 inches in diameter.

Eared Ark (*Anadara notabilis*):
South-east coast U.S.A. to Brazil.
Occurs on lower shore, in shallow water, on mud.
Shell thick, has 'squared' appearance, with curved umbones close to wide hinge, but not so close as in Blood Ark; up to 26 prominent ribs radiating from umbones to crenulated shell margin.
Exterior shell colour, brownish-white; interior, dirty-white.
Measures up to 2 inches in length.

Noah's Ark, Zebra Ark, Turkey Wing (*Arca zebra*):
East and south-east coast U.S.A. to Brazil.
Occurs on lower shore and below, in shallow water, attached by green byssus to rocks.
Shell thick, oblong-shaped, with curved umbones; long, narrow, toothed hinge. 'Folds' in shell give it a deformed appearance; numerous smooth round ribs radiating from umbones to margin with the wavy patterning give a similarity to an outstretched bird's wing.
Exterior shell colour, white with red-brown wavy, zebra-pattern bands; interior, pearly-white.
Measures up to 3 inches in length.

Noah's Ark (*Arca tetragona*):
British Isles.
Occurs on lower shore and below, on rocks.
Thick shell has approximate oblong shape, with curved widely separated umbones leaning to one side of toothed, straight hinge, giving it a deformed appearance, which also makes it difficult to

detect in rock depressions and cavities, to which it attaches by strong dark green byssus. Reticulated on surface. Prominent ridges radiate from umbones to margin.

Exterior shell colour, under periostracum, yellow with brownish-red mottling; interior white; periostracum pale brown.

Measures up to $1\frac{1}{2}$ inches in length.

Milky Ark (*Arca lactea*).
Channel Isles; south coast England.
Occurs on lower shore and below, attached to rocks and empty shells by byssus.
Shell valves less distorted, triangular, rhomboidal, umbones lean less towards one side of toothed, straight hinge; velvety hairy periostracum.
Exterior shell colour, yellowish-white under brown periostracum.
Measures up to $\frac{3}{4}$-inch in length.

DOG COCKLES (British Isles), BITTERSWEET CLAMS (U.S.A.)

As their name indicates, these bivalves have a resemblance to Cockles, although related to the Ark Shells. The hinge is curved with numerous teeth, while the ligament is external. They occur chiefly in warm waters, on sandy bottoms. The interior valves have no pallial sinus scar.

Atlantic Bittersweet (*Glycymeris undata*):
East and south-east coast U.S.A. to Brazil.
Occurs on lower shore and below, in sand.
Shell rounded, with fine ribs; the pointed beaks are central on the ligament and almost touch.
Exterior shell colour, greenish-pale brown with darker brown mottling; interior, white.
Measures up to 2 inches in diameter.

Dog Cockle, Comb-Shell (*Glycymeris glycymeris*):
British Isles.
Occurs below lower shore, on muddy or sandy gravel, living on

Dog Cockle, Comb-Shell
(*Glycymeris glycymeris*)

Pacific Coast Bittersweet
(*Glycymeris subobsoleta*)

Atlantic Bittersweet
(*Glycymeris undata*)

or just under the surface. May be secured in dredge; occasionally washed ashore after rough seas. Shell thick, almost round, equivalve; has a broad, thick, toothed hinge; the umbones are apart, but closer than in the Ark Shells.

Exterior shell colour, dull yellowish-white with irregular red-brown markings, darker brown on margin; interior, white or yellowish-white with white margin. Old shells on shore may have dark brown markings erased.

Measures up to $2\frac{1}{2}$ inches in diameter.

Pacific Coast Bittersweet (*Glycymeris subobsoleta*):
Alaska, Aleutian Islands, Pacific coast Canada and U.S.A. Occurs on lower shore and below.

Shell rounded, inequilateral, pointed beaks central on short ligament and almost touch; numerous flat ribs.

Exterior shell colour, white with brownish markings, interior, white with a brownish area.

Measures up to $\frac{3}{4}$-inch in diameter.

COCKLES

Very familiar equivalve bivalves requiring little description. When alive approximately globular, with the curved umbones, close to the toothed beak hinge and external ligament, from which radiate numerous prominent ribs. Examined side view when valves are closed bivalves are heart-shaped and alternatively called Heart Clams or Shells in the U.S.A. Not to be confused with the British Heart Cockle (*Glossus humanus*). Most species occur in mud or sand in shallow water, buried a short distance below the surface. In Europe some species are gathered for human food by digging or raking the habitat. Empty gaping or single valves are often cast ashore.

Cardium Scabrum:
British Isles, west coast Europe.
Occurs below lower shore, in muddy sand.
Shell thick, convex, has up to 28 radiating ribs with numerous small tubercles; margin narrowly crenulated.
Exterior shell colour, brownish-white, may have greyish-pink tint; interior, white sometimes brown.
Measures up to $\frac{1}{2}$-inch in length.

Common Edible Cockle (*Cardium edule*):
British Isles, west coast Europe.
Occurs on middle and lower shore, buried in muddy or gravelly sand, clean sand, also in estuaries and bays, sometimes in vast 'beds' where cultivated for human consumption.
Shell thick, globular, semi-rhomboidal, pronounced concentric ridges and up to 30 prominent radiating ribs.
Exterior shell colour, cream-white, yellowish, or pale brown; if bivalve living in brackish water exterior may have bluish tint; interior, white.
Measures up to $2\frac{1}{2}$ inches in length.

Giant Atlantic Cockle (*Dinocardium robustum*):
South-east coast U.S.A., Gulf of Mexico.
Occurs on lower shore and below, in deep water, but empty valves are washed ashore.

Shell squarish, with up to 36 large, rounded, prominent radial ribs, from umbones to crenulated valve margins.
Exterior shell colour, pale brown with darker red-brown marking; interior, pink, with pale pink or white on margin.
Measures up to 4 inches in length.

Iceland Cockle (*Clinocardium ciliatum*):
Greenland, Atlantic coast Canada, north-east coast U.S.A., Alaska, Pacific coast Canada and U.S.A.
Occurs below lower shore, in deep water.
Shell rounded, has up to 38 prominent radial ribs from umbones to crenulated valve margins; beaks lean forward.
Exterior shell colour, pale yellow-brown with darker bands; periostracum, greyish-brown.
Measures up to $2\frac{1}{4}$ inches in length.

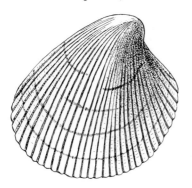

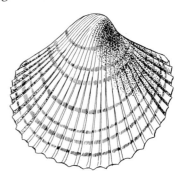

Giant Atlantic Cockle
(*Dinocardium robustum*)

Iceland Cockle
(*Clinocardium ciliatum*)

Little Cockle (*Cardium exiguum*):
British Isles.
Occurs occasionally on lower shore, but more so below, in muddy sand and fine particled mud.
Shell similar to Edible Cockle, but strongly angled, with up to 20 compressed less prominent radiating ribs, and has white 'warts' or tubercles on the anterior side ribs; crenulated margin.
Exterior shell colour, dull brownish-white or yellow with brown streaks.
Measures up to $\frac{1}{2}$-inch in length.

Nuttall's Cockle (*Clinocardium nuttalli*):
Alaska, Pacific coast Canada and U.S.A.
Occurs on lower shore and below.
Shell rounded, has up to 37 prominent radiating ribs, from umbones to crenulated margin, crossed by fine, crescent-shaped ribs; beaks lean forward.
Exterior shell colour, white, with pale brownish periostracum.
Measures up to 6 inches in length.

Prickly Cockle (*Cardium echinatum*):
British Isles; Channel Isles.
Occurs occasionally on lower shore, more so below, in sand or muddy sand.
Shell thick, with up to 20 prominent radiating ribs; exterior shell has numerous curved, backward-pointing, short, triangular spines connected at their base with a ridge, the spines reduce in size near and at the beak or umbo.
Exterior shell colour, dull whitish, yellowish or pale brown, with red-brown growth lines.
Measures up to $2\frac{1}{2}$ inches in length.

Prickly Cockle (*Trachycardium egmontianum*):
South-east coast U.S.A.
Occurs on lower shore, in sand.
Shell thick, has up to 30 prominent radiating ribs, which have numerous curved spines, from near umbones to deeply crenulated valve margin.
Exterior shell colour, white with purplish-red or purplish-brown markings; interior, purplish-red and pink, white margin.
Measures up to $2\frac{1}{2}$ inches in length.

Rough Cockle (*Cardium tuberculatum*):
South-west England, Channel Isles, south-west Ireland.
Occurs lower shore, but more so below, in sand.
Thick shell similar to Prickly Cockle (*C. echinatum*), but more globular, with up to 22 prominent but coarser ribs, the numerous tubercle-like spines being rounded, short and blunt, conical or flattened, the spines having spaces at their base, unlike *C. echinatum* where the spines are connected.
Exterior shell colour, dull white or pale brown.
Measures up to 3 inches in length.

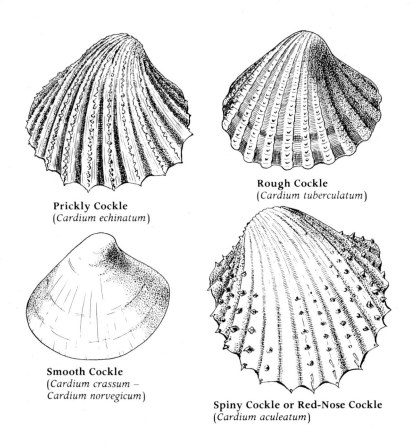

Prickly Cockle
(*Cardium echinatum*)

Rough Cockle
(*Cardium tuberculatum*)

Smooth Cockle
(*Cardium crassum –*
Cardium norvegicum)

Spiny Cockle or Red-Nose Cockle
(*Cardium aculeatum*)

Smooth Cockle (*Cardium crassum – Cardium norvegicum*):
British Isles.
Occurs below lower shore, in shell gravel and sand.
Shell is triangular and easily recognised by its exterior smoothness due to the up to 40 ribs being very low with very shallow grooves between them. The ribs almost disappear at the umbones or beaks.
Exterior shell colour, whitish or pale flesh if yellowish-green periostracum is removed by wearing.
Measures up to $2\frac{1}{4}$ inches in length.

Spiny Cockle or Red-Nose Cockle (*Cardium aculeatum*):
South-west England, Channel Isles.

Occurs below lower shore, in sand.
Shell thin, tough, has large posterior gape, up to 20 broad, radiating ribs with numerous tough, backward-pointing, curved spines; valves deeply crenulated at margin. Name is due to its bright red 'foot'. (See Red-Nose: *Hiatella striata*.)
Exterior shell colour, pale grey-brown with red-brown tints.
Measures up to 3 inches in length; the largest British cockle.

Warty Cockle (*Cardium papillosum*):
Channel Isles, Scilly Isles.
Occurs below lower shore, in sand.
Shell thick, globular, has up to 26 flat ribs with white tubercles, the narrow grooves between ribs being punctured.
Exterior shell colour, yellow, sometimes with red-brown streaks; interior, glossy, sometimes has red-brown or purple stains.
Measures up to $\frac{1}{2}$-inch in length.

Yellow Cockle (*Trachycardium muricatum*):
South-east coast U.S.A., Gulf of Mexico
Occurs on lower shore and below.
Shell nearly round, with up to 40 ribs, with a few spines; valve margin crenulated.
Exterior shell colour, creamy-yellow or brownish; interior, white or yellowish.
Measures up to 2 inches in diameter.

RAZOR SHELLS (British Isles), JACK-KNIFE AND RAZOR CLAMS (U.S.A.)

Because their valves are long, narrow and tubular this group are immediately recognisable. The hinge is at one end outside the smooth, thin, gaping valves. The genera Solen and Ensis are very similar, but Solen has one cardinal tooth on each valve; in Ensis there are two cardinal teeth on the left valve. These valves are easily damaged and single and broken valve fragments often occur on the lower shore. The bivalve mollusc lives in soft mud and sand, in which it digs downwards rapidly with its powerful 'foot' after getting a warning from approaching human feet; you must dig equally rapidly with a spade if you hope to secure it!

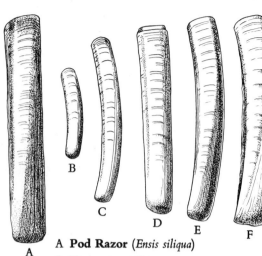

A **Pod Razor** (*Ensis siliqua*)

B **Transparent Razor**
(*Cultellus pellucidus*
Phaxas pellucidus)

C **Sword Razor** (*Ensis ensis*)

D **Grooved Razor** (*Solen marginatus*)

E **Ensis Arcuatus**

F **Atlantic Jack-Knife Clam**
(*Ensis directus*)

G **Californian Jack-Knife Cl**
(*Ensis myrae*)

The best time is as the tide returns to cover the sand and the
bivalves rise to the surface to feed and breathe, projecting the
siphon through a sand depression. In the British Isles they are
so-named because their valve shape has a similarity to the 'cut-
throat' razor; also called Spoutfish in Scotland. In the U.S.A.
they are dug for commercially and eaten as a delicacy. The
periostracum of empty valves cast ashore rapidly dries out and
peels off when exposed to sun and wind.

Atlantic Jack-Knife Clam (*Ensis directus*):
Atlantic coast Canada and U.S.A.
Occurs on lower shore, in sandy mud.
Shell valves thin, sharp-edged, slightly curved, anterior and
posterior ends truncated.
Exterior shell colour, olive and brown, with darker line or lines.
Measures up to 6 inches in length.

Californian Jack-Knife Clam (*Ensis myrae*):
Southern coast California, U.S.A.
Occurs below lower shore, in sand.
Shell valves similar in shape to Atlantic Jack-knife Clam but smaller.
Exterior shell colour, olive and brown with reddish-brown.
Measures up to 2 inches in length.

Ensis Arcuatus:
British Isles.
Occurs on lower shore, in sand.
Shell valves slightly curved, each end truncated.
Exterior shell colour, yellowish-brown with darker lines and a tapering violet-brown or whitish area.
Measures up to 6 inches in length.

Green Jack-knife Clam (*Solen viridis*):
Atlantic coast U.S.A.
Occurs on lower shore, in sand.
Shell valves thin, glossy, slightly curved, both ends truncated.
Exterior shell colour, pale and darker green.
Measures up to 2 inches in length.

Grooved Razor (*Solen marginatus*):
South-west coast England; Ireland; Scotland.
Occurs on the lower shore, in muddy sand.
Shell valves size and length equal and straight, with a deep indentation at anterior end.
Exterior shell colour, pale yellow-brown, red-brown or orange with darker markings.
Measures up to 6 inches in length.

Pod Razor (*Ensis siliqua*):
British Isles.
Occurs on lower shore, in clean sand.
Shell valves straight, each end square truncated.
Exterior shell colour, dark yellowish-brown with a tapering violet-brown or greyish area.
Measures up to $8\frac{1}{2}$ inches in length; the largest British Razor Shell.

Sword Razor (*Ensis ensis*):
British Isles, Channel Isles.
Occurs on lower shore, in sand.
Shell valves have a pronounced curve, anterior end rounded, posterior end tapered.
Exterior shell colour, yellow-brown, with a greyish-white area the length of one margin.
Measures up to 4 inches in length.

Transparent Razor (*Cultellus pellucidus – Phaxas pellucidus*):
British Isles.
Occurs below lower shore, in muddy gravel.
Shells valves curved and thin, translucent, but not transparent; posterior and anterior ends rounded.
Exterior shell colour, yellowish-white, sometimes with pink markings.
Measures up to $1\frac{1}{4}$ inches in length.

BORING BIVALVES

The shell collector will discover that there are several bivalve mollusc species which seek protection by boring into coasts formed of various types of soft rock, coral, chalk, shale, slate, stiff clay, hard and soft mud, peat, or wood objects, cement-covered pier piles and similar, even undersea cables. This activity can cause the erosion or destruction of a coastline. The first clue to it may be the finding on the shore of a piece of limestone, chalk, etc., riddled with bored, rounded holes and tunnels, which has fallen from the affected lower area of cliff, seawall and low-water mark of similar habitats. Inside this portion there may remain the valves of the mollusc responsible, but the living specimen can usually only be obtained by chiselling it carefully from the habitat. The tunnel entrance may be smaller than the interior because the latter is increased in size as the bivalve mollusc grows. The ridged valves of the majority are surprisingly thin and frail, with a pair of long, curved, blade-like processes or apophyses protruding beneath the beak within the shell valves and attached to the hinge area on to which the foot's muscles are also attached. There are numbers of accessory shell-plates between the valves on the upper surface of the living bivalves to protect valve upper margins and mantle but these are usually missing from dead examples on the shore. The valves are cut away anteriorly, so that there is a gape from which the foot protrudes. These comments apply to the Piddocks; any differences among other rock borers are detailed in the relevant description.

American Piddock (British Isles), False Angel Wing (U.S.A.) (*Petricola pholadiformis*):
Atlantic coast Canada and U.S.A., Gulf of Mexico, Caribbean, east and south coast England.
Occurs boring into stiff mud, clay, chalk, limestone and peat. As it often occurs in the vicinity of oyster 'beds' in England was possibly introduced from the U.S.A. with relaid American oysters. Similar but not related to true Angel Wings and Piddocks.
Shell elongated-oval, ridged and spined; has prominent turned-down umbones and up to 40 radiating 'ribs'; no accessory plates but has hinge teeth; ligament external behind beaks.
Exterior shell colour, chalky-white.
Measures up to $2\frac{1}{2}$ inches in length.

Angel Wing (*Barnea* [*Cyrtopleura*] *costata*):
Atlantic coast U.S.A., Caribbean to Brazil.
Occurs boring deep into mud and clay.
Shell oval, ridged; with turned-down umbones and up to 30 radiating 'ribs'; no accessory plates. Empty valves when agape resemble outstretched angels' wings or white birds' wings.
Exterior shell colour, white; periostracum, greyish; rare examples, pink.
Measures up to 8 inches in length.

Black Date Mussel (*Lithophaga nigra*):
South-east coast U.S.A., Caribbean.
Occurs boring into coral.
Shell elongated, cylindrical; prominent vertical ribs on anterior of valves.
Exterior shell colour, black; interior, whitish.
Measures up to $1\frac{1}{2}$ inches in length.

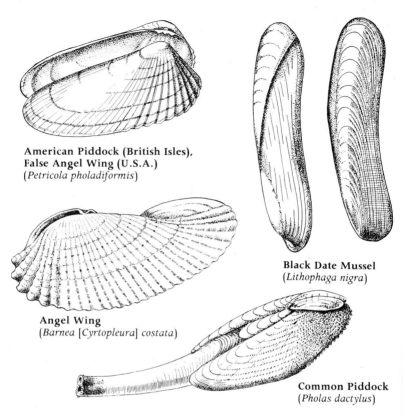

**American Piddock (British Isles),
False Angel Wing (U.S.A.)**
(*Petricola pholadiformis*)

Angel Wing
(*Barnea* [*Cyrtopleura*] *costata*)

Black Date Mussel
(*Lithophaga nigra*)

Common Piddock
(*Pholas dactylus*)

Californian Date Mussel (*Botula californiensis*):
Pacific coast Canada and U.S.A.
Occurs boring into rocks.
Shell elongated, slightly curved; smooth, with a prominent angular ridge from the beak; thick periostracum velvety, hairy at posterior.
Exterior shell colour, blackish brown.
Measures up to $1\frac{1}{2}$ inches in length.

Common Piddock (*Pholas dactylus*):
South and south-west coast England; south Wales; Ireland.
Occurs boring into chalk, red sandstone, shale, peat, submerged timber; borings may be over 12 inches long.
Shell elongated with up to 50 longitudinal rows of spines, each spine at the intersection where radiating 'ribs' and concentric

ridges join; four accessory plates, one long narrow posterior, three wider anterior.
Exterior shell colour, white; may be stained by habitat.
Measures up to 6 inches in length; largest British Piddock.

Date Mussel (*Lithophagus lithophagus*), **Rock-Borer**
(*Petricola lithophaga*):
Mediterranean.
Occurs boring in limestone.
Shell less oval than *P. pholadiformis*, shaped like a date hence its name; less prominently ribbed; periostracum very thick. Uses an acid to tunnel into the habitat, unlike other rock borers that use their shell.
Exterior shell colour, white.
Measures up to $1\frac{1}{2}$ inches in length.

Falcate Date Mussel (*Botula falcata*):
Pacific coast U.S.A.
Occurs boring into hard rock.
Shell elongated, slightly curved; with prominent angular ridge from beak; thick periostracum wrinkled.
Exterior shell colour, dark brown.
Measures up to 3 inches in length.

Fallen Angel Wing (*Barnea truncata*):
East coast U.S.A., Caribbean.
Occurs boring into clay.
Shell elongated, ridged; posterior truncated; gapes both ends.
Exterior shell colour, creamy-white; interior, white.
Measures up to 2 inches in length.

Little Piddock (*Barnea parva*):
South and south-west coast England; Channel Isles; Ireland.
Occurs boring into red sandstone, occasionally clay and limestone.
Shell oval-oblong, cut away in front, with numerous crossing, scale-like ridges, especially on anterior end of valves; hinge-plate has thick tubercle; one accessory plate; beaks closer to centre than in other piddocks.
Exterior shell colour, white, but may be stained by habitat.
Measures up to 2 inches in length.

Oval Piddock (British Isles), Great Piddock (U.S.A.)
(*Zirfaea crispata*):
Atlantic coast Canada and U.S.A.; British Isles; west coast Europe.
Occurs boring into mud, clay, shale, sand, oolite.
Shell oval, with a wide central furrow dividing valves from valve beaks to the front margins and up to 20 rows of spines, the folded hinge-plates being attached to the beaks. Very small triangular accessory plate.
Exterior shell colour, white, but may be stained by habitat.
Measures up to 2 inches in length.

Paper Piddock (*Pholadidea loscombiana*):
South and south-west coast England; west Scotland; Ireland.
Occurs boring into red sandstone, clay, peat, submerged wood.
Shell thin, partly rounded, convex, with a prominent furrow diagonally from the beaks to the margin, the upper surface being ridged. At the posterior end has a trumpet-like or cup-like membraneous extension. Two small accessory plates sometimes joined.
Exterior shell colour, white.
Measures up to $1\frac{1}{2}$ inches in length.

Red-Nose (*Hiatella striata*):
British Isles.
Occurs boring deep round tunnels into soft rocks, sandstone, limestone, chalk. Among hard rocks clings by its byssus fixed into crevices. May be attached to mussels or large lower shore seaweeds' holdfasts.
Shell approximately oblong, irregular; umbones touch; valves have a posterior gape. So-named because its two siphons have red tips and project (suggesting a red nose) from the habitat entrance. Not a Piddock or to be confused with the Red-Nose Cockle.
Exterior shell colour, dull white.
Measures up to 1 inch in length.

White Piddock (*Barnea candida*):
British Isles; Channel Isles.
Occurs boring into stiff clay, soft rock.
Shell thin, convex, elongated, almost oval, with rounded ends;

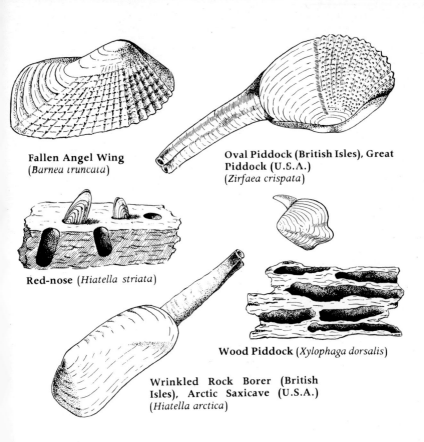

Fallen Angel Wing
(*Barnea truncata*)

Oval Piddock (British Isles), Great Piddock (U.S.A.)
(*Zirfaea crispata*)

Red-nose (*Hiatella striata*)

Wood Piddock (*Xylophaga dorsalis*)

Wrinkled Rock Borer (British Isles), Arctic Saxicave (U.S.A.)
(*Hiatella arctica*)

has up to 30 longitudinal rows of spines; one lance-shaped accessory plate, hinge-plate has single external fold.
Exterior shell colour, white.
Measures up to 3 inches in length.

Wood Piddock (*Xylophaga dorsalis*):
British Isles.
Occurs boring short spherical tunnels in floating and submerged timber, even submarine cables.
Shell globular, divided by a lengthways double ridge and furrow, posterior nearly smooth, anterior striated. Two accessory plates.
Exterior shell colour, whitish, almost transparent.
Measures up to $\frac{3}{4}$-inch in diameter.

Wrinkled Rock Borer (British Isles), Arctic Saxicave (U.S.A.) (*Hiatella arctica*):

British Isles: east coast Canada and U.S.A., Caribbean, Pacific coast Canada, U.S.A., Central America.

Occurs on lower shore and below, boring deep round tunnels into soft rocks, chalk, red sandstone and limestone. Among hard rock attaches by its byssus fixed into crevices, also attaches to large lower shore seaweeds' holdfasts; in U.S.A. habitats in or among sponges. Broken off portions of rock habitat may be found lying on shore containing living or dead molluscs inside. Shell thick, approximately oblong, irregular; wrinkled appearance due to numerous concentric ridges; umbones touch; valves have posterior gape; may have a spiny double ridge from beak near to posterior; one valve may also be larger than the other; periostracum flaky. Not a Piddock. (See Red-Nose.) May be a variant of Red-Nose or vice-versa.

Exterior shell colour, dull white.

Measures up to 2 inches in length.

4   More Bivalves

A large number of Bivalve shells are at first glance very similar, due to their rounded or near-triangular shape. The collector can make accurate identification of these if close study is given to each species' details and the type of habitat where found. In the U.S.A. many of them are named as 'Clams' and I have indicated where these have different British or European names.

ASTARTES (British Isles), ASTARTES OR CHESTNUT CLAMS (U.S.A.)

The shells of this group are tough, thick, oval or near-triangular shaped, semi-flattened, usually with pronounced concentric ribs. The exterior is covered with a thick brownish or yellow periostracum, to prevent penetration by Boring Sponges. The beaks are prominent and near these is a lunule, a depression, either lance- or heart-shaped. There are three central cardinal 'teeth' below the beak and a lateral 'tooth' on either side on the interior. As there is no siphon the interior of the valves have no pallial sinus on the pallial line. The majority frequent cooler regions in shallow or offshore deep water, the shells of some species being washed ashore.

Astarte Elliptica:
Scotland; Shetland Isles; Scandinavia; Iceland and northern regions to Greenland.
Occurs below lower shore, in deep water.
Shell very similar to Furrowed Astarte (*A. sulcata*) but posterior has more pronounced curve; up to 40 concentric ribs; ribs disappear at smooth inner margin.
Exterior shell colour, brown periostracum, white underneath this.
Measures up to an inch in length.

75

Furrowed Astarte (*Astarte sulcata*)

Striate Astarte (British Isles), Boreal Astarte (U.S.A.) (*Astarte borealis*)

Flat Astarte (*Astarte montagui*):
British Isles, Yorkshire and Antrim, Ireland, northwards; Norway.
Occurs below lower shore in deep water, in mud and sand.
Shell triangular, nearly equilateral valves; only slight depressions between ridges; close concentric ribs at umbones, but may be nearly smooth; the margins smooth, with a plain bevelled, not notched, edge.
Exterior shell colour, brown periostracum, white underneath this.
Measures up to $\frac{3}{4}$-inch in length.

Furrowed Astarte (*Astarte sulcata*):
British Isles; North Sea and Atlantic coast, Europe; Mediterranean.
Occurs below lower shore, in deep water, on sand and mud.
Shell thick, triangular, up to 40 pronounced concentric ribs; thick margin finely crenulated; hinge-plate has three cardinal 'teeth', one usually indistinct; indistinct lateral 'teeth'.
Exterior shell colour, brown periostracum, white underneath this.
Measures up to an inch in length.

Smooth Astarte (*Astarte castanea*):
Atlantic coast Canada, north-east coast U.S.A.
Occurs below lower shore, in mud.

Shell thick, rounded, the numerous concentric ribs being weak so valves nearly smooth; beaks pointed; small external ligament; inner margins finely crenulated.
Exterior shell colour, mid-brown periostracum.
Measures up to an inch in length.

Striate Astarte (British Isles), Boreal Astarte (U.S.A.) (*Astarte borealis*):
Atlantic coast Canada, north-east coast U.S.A., northern coasts British Isles.
Occurs on lower shore and below.
Shell rounded-oval, egg-shaped; numerous indistinct concentric ribs, more prominent near beak, none on valve margins, inner margins smooth, no crenulation; external ligament large.
Exterior shell colour, dark brown periostracum.
Measures up to $1\frac{1}{2}$ inches in length.

Triangular Astarte (*Astarte triangularis*):
British Isles; Channel Isles.
Occurs on lower shore and below, on sand.
Shell thick, triangular, with three almost equal sides; smooth or almost smooth with a few fine striations; margins thick and crenulated or plain, smooth and bevelled.
Exterior shell colour, yellowish or brown periostracum streaked with dark brown, white underneath this.
Measures up to $\frac{1}{4}$-inch in length.

Waved Astarte (*Astarte undata*):
Atlantic coast Canada, north-east coast U.S.A.
Occurs below lower shore, in mud.
Shell thick, up to 10 prominent, wide, concentric ribs; beaks inward curving.
Exterior shell colour, red-brown periostracum.
Measures up to $1\frac{1}{4}$ inches in length.

MISCELLANEOUS

The two following shells are not to be confused with the American Heart Shells or Iceland Cockle (See Cockles – Chapter 3.) This will be avoided if the relevant details are considered. They

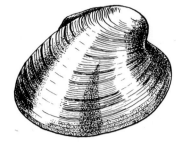

Iceland Cyprina (*Cyprina islandica*)

Heart Cockle (*Glossus humanus*)

are in the same shell sub-class as the Astartes.

Heart Cockle (*Glossus humanus*):
South-west and west coast England, west and east coast Scotland, south and east coast Ireland.
Occurs below lower shore, buried in mud with short siphons and part of shell exposed.
Shell thick, almost spherical; end view is heart-shaped; beaks twisted towards the anterior which makes it almost impossible to mistake; broad hinge-plate has two cardinal 'teeth' and two lateral 'teeth'.
Exterior shell colour, yellowish-white, but usually covered by the blackish-brown periostracum.
Measures up to 4 inches in length.

Iceland Cyprina (*Cyprina islandica*):
British Isles.
Occurs on the lower shore and below, in muddy sand or mud.
Shell thick, triangular-rounded; end view is heart-shaped; numerous irregular concentric ridges; prominent curved beaks; broad hinge-plate has three cardinal teeth.
Exterior shell colour, white, with yellow tint, but usually covered by dark brown, almost black, periostracum.
Measures up to $4\frac{1}{2}$ inches in length.

78

LUCINA (British Isles) OR LUCINES (U.S.A.) AND DOUBLE-TOOTH SHELLS (British Isles) OR DIPLODONS (U.S.A.)

The rounded, equivalve shells of the Lucina and Double-Tooths are compressed, have prominent concentric ridges or may be smooth, the umbones pointing forwards, the hinge on both valves having two cardinal 'teeth' and two lateral 'teeth'. There is no pallial sinus. In the U.S.A. the Lucina are alternatively named as White Shells, because some of the species there are that colour and have a deep groove or fold from the umbone to the shell margin. They occur on the lower shore level or below, on sand, gravel, or sandy-mud bottoms.

Californian Lucine (*Codakia californica*):
Californian coast U.S.A.
Occurs on lower shore and below, in sand.
Shell rounded, with numerous fine concentric ridges; aid to identity is lunule on right valve fits a recess in the left valve.
Exterior shell colour, brownish-white.
Measures up to an inch in diameter.

Florida Lucine (*Lucina floridana*):
South-east coast U.S.A.
Occurs on lower shore and below.
Shell almost round; smooth; with irregular concentric ridges; weak, indistinct hinge teeth; lunule small; periostracum flaky.
Exterior shell colour, dull white and brownish.
Measures up to an inch in diameter.

Northern Lucina (*Lucina* [*Phacoides*] *borealis*):
British Isles.
Occurs on lower shore and below, on sandy gravel; sometimes in beds of eel-grass.
Shell nearly rounded; swollen; has numerous low, concentric ridges or striations; margins smooth, bevelled; interior has irregular nacreous tubercles; beaks pointed; hinge teeth two cardinal 'teeth' and a lengthy lateral.
Exterior shell colour, dull chalky-white, but may have overlying

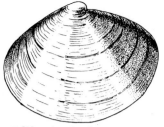

Californian Lucine
(*Codakia californica*)

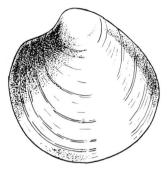

Northern Lucina
(*Lucina* [*Phacoides*] *borealis*)

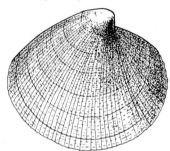

Tiger Lucine (Codakia orbicularis)

yellow-brown periostracum; interior, chalky-white.
Measures up to 1½ inches in diameter.

Pacific Orb Diplodon (*Diplodonta orbella*):
Alaska; Pacific coast Canada, U.S.A., Central America.
Occurs on lower shore and below.
Shell rounded; smooth, but with some concentric ridges; two
cardinal 'teeth' on each valve; prominent ligament, periostracum
fibrous.
Exterior shell colour, brownish-white, periostracum brown.
Measures up to ¾-inch in diameter.

Pennsylvanian Lucine (Lucina pennsylvanica):
South-east coast U.S.A., Caribbean.
Occurs on lower shore and below, in sand.
Shell thick, rounded; has numerous prominent concentric ridges;
a groove or fold from the umbone to the margin; lunule heart-
shaped.
Exterior shell colour, chalky-white; periostracum pale yellow.
Measures up to 1½ inches in diameter.

Prickly Lucina (*Lucina* [*Myrtea*] *spinifera*):
British Isles.
Occurs on lower shore and below.
Shell bluntly triangular; up to 50 fine concentric ridges, the overlapping edges creating sharp spines on the upper or dorsal margin; external ligament; beaks less prominent than in *L. borealis*; one cardinal tooth on right valve, two on left valve.
Exterior shell colour, yellowish-white; interior, may have central salmon area.
Measures up to $\frac{3}{4}$-inch in diameter.

Round Double-Tooth (*Diplodonta rotundata*):
South and west coast British Isles; south-west coast Ireland.
Occurs on lower shore and below, on muddy sand and gravel.
Shell rounded, swollen; glossy; has prominent, irregular, concentric ridges; external ligament; hinge 'teeth' two cardinal 'teeth' and two lateral 'teeth' on both valves.
Exterior shell colour, white, but yellow periostracum may partly cover this.
Measures up to an inch in diameter.

Tiger Lucine (*Codakia orbicularis*):
South-east coast U.S.A., Caribbean.
Occurs on lower shore and below, on sand.
Shell nearly round, with numerous concentric ridges crossed by numerous fine, radiating, longitudinal grooves; small lunule heart-shaped.
Exterior shell colour, brownish-white; interior, pink margins.
Measures up to 3 inches in diameter.

ARTEMIS SHELLS (British Isles),
DOSINIA SHELLS (U.S.A.)

The Artemis Shells or Dosinia Shells are members of a large family of bivalve molluscs, the Veneridae, which sometimes are extremely common on the lower shore, either as single valves or complete shells. The equivalve shells are somewhat solid, either oval or rounded, the umbones turned-in towards the anterior end. There are up to four cardinal 'teeth' on each valve, also

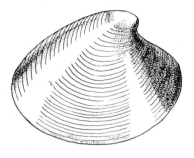

Elegant Dosinia (*Dosinia elegans*)   **Rayed Artemis** (*Dosinia exoleta*)

lateral 'teeth'. The ligament is external. The pallial line has a deep
sinus. The Artemis molluscs, with the other family members,
the Venus and Carpet molluscs, are shallow burrowers, while the
molluscs of the Tellin, Furrow, Otter and Gaper shells are deep
burrowers, in sand, gravel or muddy sand, so the latter may have
to be dug for in these habitats unless they occur as dead empty
valves.

Disc Dosinia (*Dosinia discus*):
South-east coast U.S.A.; Gulf of Mexico.
Occurs on lower shore and below, in sand.
Shell nearly round; similar to Elegant Dosinia, but smoother due
to greater number of finer concentric ridges; interior valve margin
smooth.
Exterior shell colour, white, but may have traces of the very thin
yellow periostracum.
Measures up to 3 inches in diameter.

Elegant Dosinia (*Dosinia elegans*):
South-east coast U.S.A.; Caribbean.
Occurs on lower shore and below, in sand.
Shell nearly round, with numerous concentric ridges; interior
valve margin smooth.
Exterior shell colour, white, but may have traces of very thin,
glossy, yellow periostracum.
Measures up to 3 inches in diameter.

Rayed Artemis (*Dosinia exoleta*):

British Isles.

Occurs on lower shore and below, in or on sand.

Shell nearly round, with numerous smooth, flattened, concentric ridges; bevelled margins.

Exterior shell colour, pale grey, cream or pale brownish, with several very pale ray markings of a similar or different colour from the umbones to valve margin.

Measures up to 2 inches in diameter.

Smooth Artemis (*Dosinia lupinus*):

British Isles.

Occurs on lower shore and below, in sand.

Shell similar to Rayed Artemis (*D. exoleta*), but more convex, smoother and with very numerous fine, smooth, flattened, concentric ridges; thick margins bevelled.

Exterior shell colour, white or very pale grey; sometimes with a pinkish hue and pink beaks.

Measures up to $1\frac{1}{2}$ inches in diameter.

VENUS SHELLS (British Isles), VENUS CLAMS (U.S.A.)

These shells are members of the same family, the Veneridae, as the foregoing, but have a more triangular outline, while the interior margin of the valves is variably crenulated or serrated. They have a lunule in front of the ligament.

Banded Venus (*Venus fasciata*):

British Isles.

Occurs on middle shore, lower shore and below, in sand and gravel.

Shell compressed, triangular-rounded, having numerous prominent, concentric ridges. Adult examples have fewer ridges but usually all the same size; in younger examples ridges may be alternately large and small and less in number; the interior margin of valves very finely crenulated.

Exterior shell colour, very variable, brown, red, pink, buff or yellow, sometimes white, with several darker rays, streaks or

King Venus (*Chione paphia*)

Banded Venus (*Venus fasciata*)

blotches.
Measures up to $1\frac{1}{4}$ inches in length.

Cross-Barred Venus (*Chione cancellata*):
South-east coast U.S.A.; Central America.
Occurs on lower shore and below.
Shell rounded-triangular, with numerous prominent, raised, concentric ridges and radial ribs; lunule heart-shaped.
Exterior shell colour, pale greyish-white; interior, white with a deep purple area.
Measures up to an inch in diameter.

King Venus (*Chione paphia*):
South-east coast U.S.A.; West Indies.
Occurs on lower shore and below, in sand.
Shell thick, rounded-triangular, with up to 10 thick, prominent, concentric ridges which become thin at the posterior; lunule dorsal margin curved; because of thickened ridges easy to identify.
Exterior shell colour, pale yellowish or greyish, with irregular red-brown markings; interior, white or pale yellow, with red-brown area.
Measures up to $1\frac{1}{2}$ inches in diameter.

Oval Venus (*Venus ovata*):
British Isles.
Occurs on lower shore and below, in sand.
Shell oval-triangular; equilateral; with up to 50 radiating ribs from beaks and up to 25 thin concentric striae crossing them and creating tubercles on each rib; not to be confused with Cockles; valves have crenulated interior margins.

Exterior shell colour, yellow, with red or pink tints or reddish-brown spotted.
Measures up to ¾-inch in length.

Pacific White Venus (*Amiantis callosa*):
Pacific coast California, U.S.A.; Mexico.
Occurs on lower shore and below, on sand.
Shell rounded-triangular, thick, with numerous concentric ridges; small lunule heart-shaped.
Exterior shell colour, brownish-white; interior, ivory-white.
Measures up to 3 inches in diameter.

Pale Venus (*Venus casina*):
British Isles.
Occurs on lower shore and below, in sand.
Shell is similar to Warty Venus (*V. verrucosa*), but has thick, wide, flattened, overlapping, concentric ribs or are occasionally in sharp layers; deeply scored between ribs.
Exterior shell colour, pale yellowish-white, sometimes with pale red or brown ray markings.
Measures up to 1¾ inches in length.

Royal Comb Venus (*Pitar dione*):
South-east coast U.S.A.; Gulf of Mexico; West Indies.
Occurs below lower shore.
Shell triangular-rounded, with numerous prominent, concentric ridges; the posterior has several long and short pointed spines, with a resemblance to widely-spaced teeth of a comb, hence its name. Once widely collected and now scarce.
Exterior shell colour, ivory-white, base of spines purple and violet.
Measures up to 2 inches in length excluding spines.

Striped Venus (*Venus striatula* [*gallina*]):
British Isles; North Sea, Europe, coasts.
Occurs on lower shore and below, in sand.
Shell triangular and semi-convex; numerous overlapping, concentric ribs which close together on either side; interior margin of valves finely crenulated.
Exterior shell colour, pale yellow, with three reddish-brown

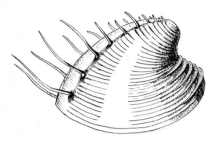

Royal Comb Venus (*Pitar dione*)

Striped Venus
(*Venus striatula* [*gallina*])

Warty Venus, European Venus
(*Venus verrucosa*)

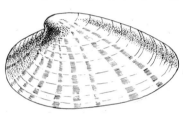

Sunray Venus
(*Macrocallista nimbosa*)

rays or broken spot markings from the beak.
Measures up to $1\frac{1}{4}$ inches in length.

Sunray Venus (*Macrocallista nimbosa*):
East and south-east coast U.S.A.; Gulf of Mexico.
Occurs on lower shore and below, in muddy sand.
Shell elongated, rounded, compressed, smooth, glossy; beaks
close to anterior; left valve has an anterior lateral tooth; perio-
stracum thin.
Exterior shell colour, greyish-lavender with darker brownish
radiating ray markings; interior, whitish.
Measures up to 5 inches in length.

Warty Venus, European Venus (*Venus verrucosa*):
South-west coast England; Wales; west coast Scotland; Channel
Isles; south and west coast Ireland; Europe coast.
Occurs below lower shore, in shell debris, gravel and sand.

Dead or empty examples occasionally washed ashore.

Shell very thick, heavy, rounded, convex; coarse-looking with thick, close-set, concentric ridges, layered at equal distances apart and forming tubercles or irregular 'warts', particularly on the hind area; interior margin of valves finely crenulated.

Exterior shell colour, dull, pale yellowish-brown, occasionally has several darker ray markings.

Measures up to 2 inches in length.

QUAHOGS OR HARD-SHELL CLAMS

These bivalve molluscs occur in the New World or tropical regions, where they are eaten. One species, the Northern Quahog, has been experimentally introduced into British coastal areas. They are members of the family Veneridae. The coastal American Indians, who called them Quahogs, not only relished them as food, but prized the shells to make 'wampum' beads. This was done by breaking the valves, chipping out the rough shape, filing smooth, then drilling through the hole to create the quarter-inch long, tubular, white or purple beads. These were woven into belts or strung together in strands. The belts had various patterns recording important Indian events of the time they were made which could be 'read' for their sign information years afterwards. They sealed treaties, while the short strands of 'wampum' beads were used instead of money to trade for goods. Purple 'wampum' is of a higher value because the Quahog valves have only small areas of purple on their interior, most of it being white.

Northern Quahog, Hard-Shell Clam, East Coast Clam, Round Clam, Littleneck Clam, Cherrystone Clam
(*Mercenaria* [*Venus*] *mercenaria*):
East coast Canada and U.S.A., California coast U.S.A.; various harbours and river mouths in southern England.

Occurs on lower shore and below, in sand or mud.

Shell thick, rounded-triangular, with numerous close, concentric ridges, apart from the middle of the exterior valve area which is smooth.

Exterior shell colour, dull brownish-grey or whitish-brown and

Northern Quahog, Hard-Shell Clam, East Coast Clam, Round Clam, Littleneck Clam, Cherry-stone Clam (*Mercenaria* [*Venus*] *mercenaria*)

may have brownish irregular markings; interior, white with purple areas near margin.
Measures up to 4 inches in width.

Southern Quahog (*Mercenaria campechiensis*):
East and south-east coast U.S.A.
Occurs on lower shore and below, in sand and mud.
Shell similar to Northern Quahog, but larger, and does not have the smooth area on middle of the exterior valves.
Exterior shell colour, brownish-white; interior white.
Measures up to 5 inches in width.

CARPET SHELLS

These are also members of the family Veneridae and are so-named because the colour patterning has a supposed resemblance to the underside of a carpet or tapestry. This is particularly applicable to the Cross-Cut Carpet Shell. They differ from Dosinia and Venus by being rhomboidal, not triangular, in shape, with the posterior end wedge-shaped. The beaks or umbones are positioned nearer the anterior end and there is no lunule. The interior margin of the valves is smooth, not crenulated.

Banded Carpet Shell (*Venerupis rhomboides* [*Tapes or Paphia virginea*]):
British Isles.
Occurs below lower shore, in shell debris, gravel, but empty valves are cast ashore.
Shell oblong, convex, glossy; with flattened concentric ridges

which may not be present on umbones.

Exterior shell colour, pale greyish-white or yellow, with zig-zag or irregular purplish-brown spots and blotch markings; interior, glossy, has purple, orange or yellow tint.

Measures up to $2\frac{1}{2}$ inches in length.

Banded Carpet Shell (*Venerupis saxatilis* [*Tapes or Paphia perforans*]):

South coast England.

Occurs in rock crevices or in empty holes previously made by rock-boring bivalves, *Pholas*, *Barnea*, *Hiatella*, etc., or may be attached to rocks by byssus threads.

Shell similar to Pullet Carpet Shell, but smaller, usually irregular and appearing distorted in shape; anterior margin may be truncated.

Exterior shell colour, pale yellowish-white with variable irregular purplish-brown markings.

Measures up to $1\frac{1}{2}$ inches in length.

Cross-Cut Carpet Shell (*Venerupis* [*Tapes or Paphia*] *decussata*):

South-west coast England.

Occurs on lower shore, in sand and muddy gravel.

Shell similar to Pullet Carpet Shell but more squarish in outline; has numerous, prominent, coarse, concentric ridges which are crossed and broken from beaks by wavy, radiating ribs, with a tuberculated posterior. Exterior shell colour, dull yellowish with irregular dark brown or purple markings.

Measures up to 2 inches in length.

Golden Carpet Shell (*Venerupis* [*Tapes*] *aurea*):

South-west coast England; Wales; west coast Scotland; Ireland.

Occurs on lower shore and below, in sand and gravel.

Shell triangular, convex, with flattened, shallow, concentric growth bands; margins plain.

Exterior shell colour, uniform golden-yellow or pale yellowish-white, sometimes with irregular patterning of purple or reddish-brown.

Measures up to $1\frac{1}{2}$ inches in length.

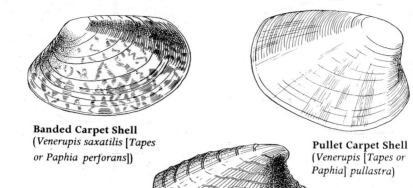

Banded Carpet Shell
(*Venerupis saxatilis* [*Tapes or Paphia perforans*])

Pullet Carpet Shell
(*Venerupis* [*Tapes or Paphia*] *pullastra*)

Rock Venus
(*Venerupis* [*Irus*] *irus*)

Pullet Carpet Shell (*Venerupis* [*Tapes or Paphia*] *pullastra*):
British Isles.

Occurs on the lower shore and below, in muddy gravel and sand, but may also be attached by byssus threads to or in empty shells, rocks and similar objects, or to the holdfasts of Laminaria seaweed.

Shell rhomboidal, similar to Cross-Cut Carpet Shell, but only finely ridged with close concentric, flattened bands, which are layered on the posterior, and longitudinal striae from the beaks to the margins.

Exterior shell colour, yellowish-white, with variable, irregular markings of red-brown or purple-brown, which in some examples suggests the plumage of a pullet, hence its name.

Measures up to $2\frac{1}{2}$ inches in length.

Rock Venus (*Venerupis* [*Irus*] *irus*):
Channel Isles; Ireland; Scilly Isles; south-west coast England; south coast Wales.

Occurs on limestone rocks in holes created by Hiatella, Pholas, in rock crevices, or among holdfasts of Laminaria seaweed. Shell different from relatives, oblong; up to 15 thin, concentric ridges, with edges toothed and with fine striae from the beaks. Due to continued existence in habitat shell may be distorted.

Exterior shell colour, white, sometimes blotched with purple or reddish-brown.

Measures up to an inch in length.

DONAX OR WEDGE SHELLS

The Donax or Wedge Shells are found chiefly in sandy habitats and are sometimes very common. The compressed, inequilateral, glossy valves are elongated, have their beaks behind the middle line, the interior margins of the valves being crenulated so that the valves interlock when closed. The left valve has two cardinal 'teeth', the right valve has a double central 'tooth', there being a lateral 'tooth' fore and aft in each valve. The valves, when the mollusc is dead, often remain hinged together and following a storm numerous examples are discovered cast ashore, where they lie open like butterflies with wings expanded. The Donax molluscs are shallow burrowers in the habitat.

Banded Wedge Shell (*Donax vittatus*):
British Isles.
Occurs on middle shore, lower shore and below, in large, exposed, sandy habitats.
Shell inequilateral, wedge-shaped, anterior region larger; glossy; with numerous fine, radiating grooves; interior margin prominently crenulated.
Exterior shell colour, very variable and bright, ground-yellow, brown, olive, purple, violet and may have from beaks three white or pale rays, concentric bands sometimes of a deeper shade than ground colour; interior sometimes has violet blotches or spots.
Measures up to 1½ inches in length, an inch broad.

Californian Donax or Wedge Clam (*Donax californicus*):
Californian coast U.S.A.; Central America.
Occurs on lower shore, especially in sandy bays.
Shell thin, elongated-triangular, with fine, radiating grooves.
Exterior shell colour, yellowish-white and may have indistinct ray markings; interior, white with purple area or hue; periostracum, brownish to greenish.
Measures up to an inch in length.

Florida Coquina (*Donax variabilis*):
East and south-east coast U.S.A.
Occurs on the lower shore.

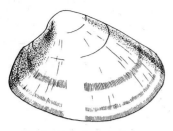

Banded Wedge Shell
(*Donax vittatus*)

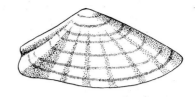

Californian Donax or Wedge Clam
(*Donax californicus*)

Florida Coquina (*Donax variabilis*)

Shell elongated-triangular, anterior region larger, rounded; with numerous fine, radiating striations that are more prominent on posterior.

Exterior shell colour, very variable, white, yellow, pale brown, orange, pink, red, bluish, mauve, purple, with darker radiating rays.

Measures up to ½-inch in length.

Donax Variegatus:
Channel Isles; south-west coast England.
Occurs on lower shore and below, in sand.
Shell similar to Banded Wedge Shell, but more oblong and flatter; very glossy; interior margin finely crenulated or smooth.
Exterior shell colour, red-brown and creamy-white, having a prominent, wide whitish ray marking from the beak to the margin.
Measures up to 1¼ inches in length.

TELLIN SHELLS

The Tellins are a very large family of deep burrowing bivalve molluscs, some of which have very beautiful and colourful shells. The shell shape is rounded elongated or oval and very compressed to allow quick progression through the habitat, usually mud or sand. They are thin and in some cases fragile, the hinge, with two cardinal 'teeth', being weak, so empty examples cast ashore may be separated or fragmented.

Baltic Tellin (British Isles) (*Macoma* [*Tellina*] *balthica*),
Balthic Macoma (U.S.A.) (*Macoma balthica*):
British Isles; western Baltic Sea, hence its name, but despite this also found on North Sea, North Atlantic and Mediterranean coasts; Arctic coast Canada; Pacific coast Canada and U.S.A.
Occurs on lower shore and below, frequently in estuaries, in muddy sandy gravel.
Shell more globular than other relatives, but triangular-rounded in side outline; with fine, irregular, concentric striations; periostracum thin.
Exterior shell colour, variable, white, yellow to crimson and purplish, sometimes with concentric bands of a deeper hue; interior may be pink.
Measures up to an inch in length.

Bean-like Tellin (*Tellina fabula*):
British Isles; North Sea, Europe, coasts.
Occurs on lower shore and below, in sand.
Shell thin, triangular-oval or oblong; translucent; glossy. Similar to Thin Tellin but right valve only has fine diagonal striations that identifies it from T. tenuis.
Exterior shell colour, pearl-white, but may have yellowish tint.
Measures up to $\frac{3}{4}$-inch in length.

Blunt Tellin (*Tellina crassa*):
British Isles.
Occurs below lower shore, in shell debris, sand and gravel.
Shell rounded, thick; with numerous fine, concentric ribs; in-equivalve, left valve slightly larger and more compressed than right valve.
Exterior shell colour, yellowish-white with pale pink rays or variegations from beak to margin; interior may be orange.
Measures up to $2\frac{1}{4}$ inches in length.

Candy-Stick Tellin (*Tellina similis*):
South-east coast U.S.A.; Caribbean.
Occurs on lower shore and below, in sand.

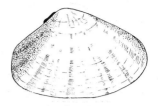

Candy-Stick Tellin
(*Tellina similis*)

Baltic Tellin (British Isles)
(*Macoma* [*Tellina*] *balthica*),
Balthic Macoma (U.S.A.)
(*Macoma balthica*)

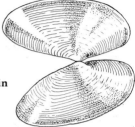

Donax-like Tellin, Hatchet Tellin
(*Tellin donacina*)

Shell thin, compressed, elongated triangular-rounded, with numerous fine, concentric ridges.

Exterior shell colour, white, sometimes a pale yellow area, with up to 12 red ray markings from beak to margin, although in some examples red rays may only be around margin; interior, white with rays near margin only.

Measures up to an inch in length.

Donax-like Tellin, Hatchet Tellin (*Tellina donacina*):
Mediterranean; Europe coast; British Isles; Ireland.
Occurs below lower shore, in shell debris and gravel.
Shell angular-oblong and similar to Donax, but occurs in a different habitat; compressed; has numerous, fine, concentric striae.
Exterior shell colour, yellowish-white with prominent pink ray markings or pink blotch markings.
Measures up to an inch in length.

Little Tellin (*Tellina pygmaea*):
British Isles; North Sea coasts; France; Channel Isles.
Occurs on lower shore and below, in sand.
Shell similar to Donax-like Tellin, but smaller, more convex; very fine striae; posterior rounded and truncated.

Exterior shell colour, bright yellow, white, pink, rose-red, orange; usually with rays of a different or deeper tint.
Measures up to $\frac{1}{2}$-inch in length.

Rose-Petal Tellin (*Tellina lineata*):
South-east coast U.S.A.; Caribbean.
Occurs on lower shore and below, in sand.
Shell triangular-rounded, glossy, smooth, with fine, concentric ridges.
Exterior shell colour, variable, white to delicate rose-pink; interior, same, but pink examples may have whitish margin.
Measures up to an inch in length.

Rough Tellin (*Tellina squalida*):
Channel Isles; south and west coast England; Ireland.
Occurs below lower shore, in sand.
Shell triangular-rounded, flattened, slightly inequivalve; with numerous thin, concentric striae, but the posterior has slanting striae, giving it a rough appearance.
Exterior shell colour, satiny, yellow or pale orange, with a reddish tint close to the beaks; may also have lighter bands.
Measures up to $1\frac{3}{4}$ inches in length.

Salmon Tellin (*Tellina salmonea*):
Alaska; Pacific coast Canada and U.S.A.
Occurs on lower shore and below, in sand.
Shell triangular-rounded; glossy; smooth, with several growth lines.
Exterior shell colour, white, the growth lines being dark, usually brownish; interior, salmon-pink.
Measures up to $\frac{1}{2}$-inch in length.

Speckled Tellin (*Tellina listeri*):
East and south coast U.S.A.; Central America.
Occurs on lower shore and below, in sand.
Shell elongated, with numerous concentric ridges which are evenly spaced.
Exterior shell colour, white, with brown irregular, 'speckled' markings from beak to margin.
Measures up to 3 inches in length.

Sunrise Tellin (*Tellina radiata*)

Thin Tellin (*Tellina tenuis*)

Sunrise Tellin (*Tellina radiata*):
South-east coast U.S.A.; Caribbean; West Indies.
Occurs on lower shore and below, in sand.
Shell thin, elongated triangular-oval; smooth, very glossy.
Exterior shell colour, pale yellow, with wide mauve-pink ray markings from beak to margin, giving an appearance of the sun's rays over the horizon at sunrise; occasionally yellow and white, rarely entirely white; interior, yellow and mauve-pink.
Measures up to 3 inches in length.

Thin Tellin (*Tellina tenuis*):
British Isles.
Occurs middle shore, lower shore and below, in clean sand.
Shell triangular-oval; thin; very flattened; glossy; translucent; ligament tough, so empty valves are more frequently found united than is usual in Tellins.
Exterior shell colour, variable, white, yellow, to frequently rose-pink; interior, same.
Measures up to $\frac{3}{4}$-inch in length.

MACOMA SHELLS OR CLAMS

The Macoma Shells are found on the United States coastline, only two species, the Baltic Macoma and Chalky Macoma, occurring in the British Isles. They are more globular than the Tellins and triangular-rounded, with an obvious posterior 'twist' and do not have lateral 'teeth'. Although chiefly white they often have remnants of the brownish periostracum remaining. Macomas occur in muddy habitats, usually in cool regions, some species being gathered for human consumption.

Atlantic Grooved Macoma (*Psammotreta intastriata*):
South-east coast U.S.A.; Caribbean.
Occurs on lower shore and below, in mud.
Shell thin, triangular-rounded, with a very clear posterior twist;
left valve has a radial groove, right valve posterior radial rib.
Exterior shell colour, dull brownish-white; interior white.
Measures up to 2 inches in length.

Balthic Macoma (See Baltic Tellin in Tellin section).

Bent-Nose Macoma (*Macoma nasuta*):
Alaska; Pacific coast Canada and U.S.A.
Occurs on lower shore and below, especially in calm bays, in mud.
Shell triangular-rounded; similar to the White Sand Macoma, but
differs by the pallial sinus on the left valve joining the anterior
muscle scar.
Exterior shell colour, white, with remnants of brownish perio-
stracum forming edge to the margin.
Measures up to $3\frac{1}{2}$ inches in width.

Chalky Macoma (*Macoma calcarea*):
Northern coast British Isles; Scandinavia; east coast Canada and
north-east coast U.S.A.; Pacific coast Canada and U.S.A.
Occurs on lower shore and below, in mud.
Shell triangular-rounded, with concentric ridges; similar to
Baltic Macoma, but longer and larger.
Exterior shell colour, white, with remnants of brownish
periostracum near and on margin.
Measures up to $1\frac{3}{4}$ inches in length.

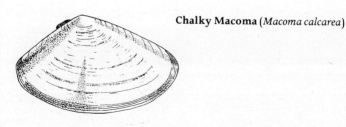

Chalky Macoma (*Macoma calcarea*)

White Sand Macoma (*Macoma secta*):
Pacific coast Canada and U.S.A.
Occurs on lower shore and below, in muddy sand.
Shell thin, triangular-rounded; left valve flattened; short ligament partly internal.
Exterior shell colour, white or creamy, sometimes with margin covered with brown periostracum.
Measures up to 3 inches in length.

FURROW SHELLS

This family is so-named because the ligament pit or chondrophore, a narrow opening under the beak, is spoon-shaped. The Furrow Shells are similar to the Tellins, except that their hinge 'teeth' comprise two cardinal 'teeth' on the right valve, one cardinal 'tooth' on the left valve and no lateral 'teeth'. The Tellins have an external ligament, the Furrow Shells an internal ligament. There is a gape for the extension of the siphons. They are deep burrowers. A clue to their presence is the radiating pattern of grooves in the mud surface around the point where the inhalant siphon emerged, made by the siphon drawing in the organic deposit. It has been suggested that the family name may have originated from these groove patterns.

Glossy Furrow Shell (*Abra nitida*):
British Isles.
Occurs below lower shore, in muddy sand.
Shell similar to Prismatic Furrow Shell, but more oval, bean-shaped, nearly flat; posterior margins curved; has concentric ridges.
Exterior shell colour, white.
Measures up to $\frac{3}{4}$-inch in length.

Peppery Furrow Shell (*Scrobicularia plana*):
British Isles.
Occurs on lower shore and below, in mud, muddy sand or clay; also occurring in estuaries, creeks in salt marshes, buried up to a depth of 12 inches or more.
Shell thin, rounded-oval; very flat; has some concentric ridges.

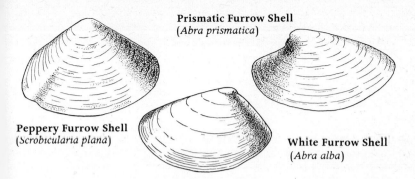

Prismatic Furrow Shell
(*Abra prismatica*)

Peppery Furrow Shell
(*Scrobicularia plana*)

White Furrow Shell
(*Abra alba*)

Exterior shell colour, greyish-white or pale yellowish-brown, but may be stained by habitat material.
Measures up to 2 inches in length.

Prismatic Furrow Shell (*Abra prismatica*):
British Isles.
Occurs below lower shore, in sand.
Shell thin, frail, oblong, wedge-shaped; nearly flat; with fine striae; translucent, polished with a prismatic quality caused by the thin layer of the periostracum.
Exterior shell colour, pearly-white.
Measures up to $\frac{3}{4}$-inch in length.

White Furrow Shell (*Abra alba*):
British Isles; North Sea coasts Europe.
Occurs on lower shore and below, in mud, also estuaries, bays, creeks and tidal inlets.
Shell thin, oval, with fine, concentric ridges; highly polished.
Exterior shell colour, opaque white.
Measures up to $\frac{3}{4}$-inch in length.

SUNSET SHELLS (British Isles),
SUNSET CLAMS (U.S.A.)

These elongated, slender, compressed shells are not as beautiful as their name might suggest. It was given because the radiating rays on the shell have a supposed resemblance to rays appearing on the horizon as the sun sinks below it. Although related to the

Tellins there is no posterior twist to the valves of the Sunset Shells as in the similar Macomas. They are shallow burrowers in the habitat.

Californian Sunset Clam (*Gari californica*):
Alaska; Pacific coast Canada and U.S.A.
Occurs on lower shore and below, in sandy mud.
Shell oval-rounded posterior slightly truncated; with numerous, prominent, irregular, concentric ridges; the large ligament is sited over the hinge.
Exterior shell colour, whitish-yellow, with radiating pinkish-red or purplish ray markings or similar tinted areas; remnants of dark periostracum may be on valve margins; interior, white.
Measures up to 3 inches in length.

Faroe Sunset Shell (*Gari fervensis*):
British Isles.
Occurs on lower shore and below, in sand.
Shell oblong, almost equilateral; compressed; with numerous, prominent, fine, concentric ridges; several radiating ribs from the beaks; posterior truncated; posterior ribs keeled.
Exterior shell colour, pink, with sometimes indistinct, radiating white, yellowish or darker pink rays; may also be small white spots; in some examples greenish periostracum may survive to cover parts of the exterior surface; occasionally specimens are a purplish hue; interior, purple, polished.
Measures up to $1\frac{3}{4}$ inches in length.

Large Sunset Shell (*Gari depressa*):
South-west coast England; Ireland; West Scotland.
Occurs below lower shore, in sand.
Shell oval, compressed; has numerous faint concentric ridges near margins which look as if they have been worn off the shell surface.
Exterior shell colour, yellowish-white, with lilac or purple-brown rays; may have patchy areas of olive-brown periostracum remaining; interior, yellow, with purple hue near beak or entire interior purplish.
Measures up to $2\frac{1}{4}$ inches in length.

Californian Sunset Clam
(*Gari californica*)

Faroe Sunset Shell
(*Gari fervensis*)

Tellin-like Sunset Shell
(*Gari tellinella*)

Ribbed Sunset Shell (*Gari costulata*):
South-west coast England; Wales; west Scotland; south and
west coast Ireland.
Occurs below lower shore, in sand.
Shell compressed; inequivalve; similar to the Tellin-like Sunset
Shell, but has up to 20 sharp ribs on posterior slope, radiating
from the beaks to the margin: due to these ribs contrasting
markedly with the smooth-surfaced remainder of the shell it
was given its name.
Exterior shell colour, yellowish-white, with deep purple rays.
Measures up to an inch in length.

Tellin-like Sunset Shell (*Gari tellinella*):
British Isles.
Occurs on lower shore and below, in sand.
Shell oblong; thin, compressed; glossy; with numerous fine
concentric ribs.
Exterior shell colour, yellowish-white, with a flame-red or
purple tint; the radiating rays or streaks are either pink, flame-
red, violet or purple; may also be similar short streaks or longer
streaks close to the beaks on upper edge of the valves; interior,
similar coloration, polished.
Measures up to $1\frac{1}{4}$ inches in length.

SURF CLAMS (U.S.A.),
TROUGH SHELLS (British Isles)

These bivalves' shells are to be found in clean sand, shell debris and gravel, not mud. In the U.S.A. they are called Surf Clams because the molluscs there favour a surf environment on the shore. They are shallow burrowers in the habitat. The shells are equivalve and equilateral, triangular oval or elliptical in shape and heterodont. Each valve has two cardinal 'teeth', which in the left valve are joined in an erection like an inverted V. The right valve has four large lateral 'teeth' and the left valve two laterals. On the hinge is a spoon-shaped depression or chondrophore containing the resilium or horny pad which maintains the narrow gape of the valves. Several of the larger species are edible and are harvested commercially.

Atlantic Surf Clam (*Spisula solidissima*):
East coast Canada and U.S.A.
Occurs on lower shore and below, in sand.
Shell thick, triangular-oval; with numerous fine, concentric ridges; thin periostracum.
Exterior shell colour, brownish-white or creamy; periostracum, yellowish; interior, tan.
Measures up to 7 inches in length.

Cut Trough Shell (*Spisula subtruncata*):
British Isles; Ireland; North Sea coasts Europe.
Occurs below lower shore, in sand.
Shell strongly angular; convex; ends of valves contracted; depression either side of beaks; umbones prominent; smooth surface striated; lateral teeth finely, vertically serrated.
Exterior shell colour, whitish.
Measures up to $1\frac{1}{4}$ inches in length.

Elliptical Trough Shell (*Spisula elliptica*):
British Isles.
Occurs below lower shore, in sand, shell debris, gravel.
Shell elliptical; thin; glossy; almost smooth; dorsal area smooth, which identifies it from the Thick Trough Shell; lateral 'teeth'

finely vertically serrated.
Exterior shell colour, whitish.
Measures up to $1\frac{3}{4}$ inches in length.

Fragile Atlantic Mactra (*Mactra fragilis*):
East and south-east coast U.S.A.; Caribbean.
Occurs on lower shore and below, in sand.
Shell thin, triangular-oval; some concentric ridges, posterior has two ridges.
Exterior shell colour, yellowish; periostracum, greyish; interior, white.
Measures up to $2\frac{1}{2}$ inches in length.

Glaucous Trough Shell (*Mactra glauca*):
Channel Isles; occasionally Cornwall coast England.
Occurs on lower shore and below, in sand.
Shell triangular-oval; convex; thin; glossy; lateral 'teeth' smooth, plain, no serrations.
Exterior shell colour, yellowish-white, with yellowish-brown, pale brown or fawn rays, dorsal margin having chestnut-brown markings; may be entirely covered with pale brown satiny periostracum.
Measures up to 4 inches in length.

Rayed Trough Shell (*Mactra corallina*):
British Isles.
Occurs on lower shore and below, in clean sand.
Shell thin; triangular-rounded; glossy; lateral teeth smooth, plain, no serrations.
Exterior shell colour, yellowish-white, with pale reddish-brown, sometimes broken, rays from umbones to margins; purplish-red beaks.
Measures up to 2 inches in length.

Thick Trough Shell (*Spisula solida*):
British Isles.
Occurs on the lower shore and below, in sand.
Shell thick, triangular; smooth concentric grooves; dorsal area has a fan-shaped ridge pattern which distinguishes it from the

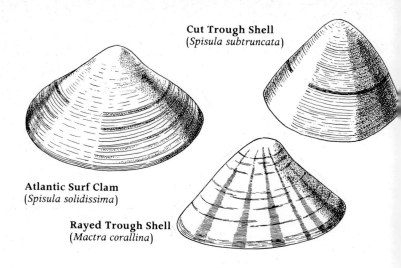

Cut Trough Shell
(*Spisula subtruncata*)

Atlantic Surf Clam
(*Spisula solidissima*)

Rayed Trough Shell
(*Mactra corallina*)

Elliptical Trough Shell; lateral 'teeth' finely vertically serrated.
Exterior shell colour, yellowish-white.
Measures up to 1½ inches in length.

OTTER SHELLS

These large shells have hinge 'teeth' similar to those of the
Trough Shells, with an apophysis in the valves where the short
partly-external ligament is attached. In the left valve the double
cardinal fits into the notch of the opposite valve created by two
large cardinal 'teeth'. The shell valves gape equally wide at both
ends. The Otter Shells are deep burrowers, vertically into mud,
up to 24 inches.

Common Otter Shell (*Lutraria lutraria* [*elliptica*]):
British Isles; Channel Isles.
Occurs on the lower shore and below, in sand, muddy sand and
soft mud.
Shell elliptical; glossy; flattened; thin but strong; two lateral
'teeth' on left valve, one lateral 'tooth' on right valve.
Exterior shell colour, yellowish-white, but may be covered or
partly so by olive-brown periostracum.
Measures up to 6 inches in length.

Otter Shells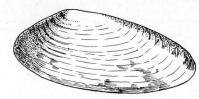

Lutraria Magna:
Channel Isles; south-west England.
Occurs on lower shore, in mud.
Shell elongated; umbo positioned forward; posterior dorsal margin either straight or concave and the posterior upcurved.
Exterior shell colour, yellowish-white, but may have remnants of dark brown periostracum.
Measures up to 4 inches in length.

GAPERS (British Isles),
SOFT-SHELL CLAMS (U.S.A.)

As their name indicates, the living Gaper mollusc has a large oval shell which, due to the extension of the long, large siphons, gapes widely at the posterior end. The left valve has a prominent large spoon-shaped chondrophore projecting from beneath the beak; in this apophysis the ligament is internal. They are deep burrowers in sand, gravel or mud, up to a depth of 12 inches. In the U.S.A. the Sand Gaper or Soft-Shell Clam is eaten as a popular delicacy, and is dug for at low water.

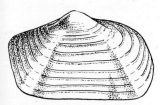

Blunt Gaper (British Isles)
(*Mya truncata*),
Truncate Soft-Shell Clam (U.S.A.)
(*Mya truncata*)

Sand Gaper (British Isles)
(*Mya arenaria*),
Soft-Shell Clam (U.S.A.)
(*Mya arenaria*)

Blunt Gaper (British Isles) (*Mya truncata*), **Truncate Soft-Shell Clam (U.S.A.)** (*Mya truncata*):
British Isles; east coast Canada, north-east coast U.S.A.

Occurs on lower shore and below, in muddy sand, gravel, clay. Shell has posterior truncated, blunted, almost straight as if damaged or broken off; anterior rounded; irregular concentric ridges; gapes wide at posterior but little at anterior end. The pallial sinus is a U-shape.

Exterior shell colour, dull greyish-white, but may be covered with brown periostracum.

Measures up to 3 inches in length.

Sand Gaper (British Isles) (*Mya arenaria*), **Soft-Shell Clam (U.S.A.)** (*Mya arenaria*):

British Isles; east coast Canada and U.S.A.; Pacific coast U.S.A. Occurs on lower shore and below, in mud, sandy mud and gravel; favours estuaries.

Shell oval-elliptical; posterior rounded and wedge-shaped; left valve flatter; has irregular, concentric ridges; gapes wide at both ends; The pallial sinus is a V-shape.

Exterior shell colour, greyish-white or brownish, may be rust-brown near beaks and may have remnants of brown periostracum.

Measures up to 5 inches in length.

BASKET SHELLS

Although other shells are inequivalve this fact is quickly realised when the complete Basket Shells are secured. The right valve is considerably larger and the smaller left valve fits tightly inside it like an operculum. The shell is also extended to cover the short siphons. The mollusc is a shallow burrower in the habitat.

Common Basket Shell
(*Corbula gibba*)

Common Basket Shell (*Corbula gibba*):
British Isles.

Occurs below lower shore, in muddy gravel and sand.

Shell triangular; smaller left valve outer margin has greyish, horny, not calcified periostracum fringe to allow it to fit securely inside right valve; valves have some concentric ridges but left

valve has only several radiating ribs; right valve of young examples may also have up to 5 spines near the beak.
Exterior shell colour, white, with yellow, reddish-brown or a pink tinge.
Measures up to $\frac{1}{2}$-inch in length.

PANDORA SHELLS (British Isles), PANDORA CLAMS (U.S.A.)

These shells are also inequivalve and inequilateral; a fact immediately noticeable, too, the left valve being convex and overlapping the flat right valve. The posterior end is also extended or sometimes upcurved. When the shell surface is worn away a nacreous layer is revealed. They do not burrow into the habitat, having very short siphons.

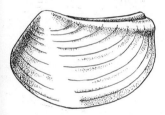

Gould's Pandora Clam
(*Pandora gouldiana*)

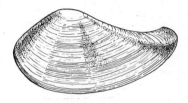

Pandora Shell
(*Pandora albida* [*inaequivalvis*])

Gould's Pandora Clam (*Pandora gouldiana*):
East coast Canada, north-east coast U.S.A.
Occurs on lower shore and below, in sand.
Shell thin, oval-elongated; posterior truncated and upcurved; numerous irregular, concentric ridges.
Exterior shell colour, chalky-white; interior, white.
Measures up to $1\frac{1}{4}$ inches in length.

Pandora Shell (*Pandora albida* [*inaequivalvis*]):
Channel Isles; south-west England.
Occurs on the lower shore and below, on sand or muddy sand surface, in shallow, sheltered bays.
Shell thin, oval-elongated; posterior dorsal line concave; each

107

valve has a cardinal 'tooth', which is horizontal on the left valve, upright on the right valve. The left valve hinge-plate has a rib which fits a notch on the right valve.

Exterior shell colour, pearly-white, may have a yellowish tint.

Measures up to $1\frac{1}{2}$ inches in length.

Pandora Pinna:
British Isles.

Occurs below lower shore, on sand.

Shell thin, similar to *Pandora albida*, but has straight posterior dorsal line.

Exterior shell colour, white.

Measures up to $\frac{3}{4}$-inch in length.

LANTERN SHELLS OR THRACIAS

These molluscs are related to the Pandoras. The fragile shells are almost oval or rounded-triangular, thin, flattened and have a posterior gape for the extension of the long siphons. They usually inhabit deep water, though the empty valves may be found closer inshore.

Common Pacific Thracia (*Thracia trapezoides*):
Alaska; Pacific coast Canada and U.S.A.

Occurs below lower shore, in sand.

Shell similar to Conrad's Thracia but more elongated; with an oblique ridge from the beak to posterior end; right beak has a hole punctured by the left beak.

Exterior shell colour, greyish.

Measures up to 2 inches in length.

Conrad's Thracia (*Thracia conradi*):
East coast Canada, north-east coast U.S.A.

Occurs on lower shore and below, in mud.

Shell rounded-triangular; irregular outline, with numerous irregular, concentric ridges; hinge teethless; the right beak with a hole punctured by the left beak.

Exterior shell colour, brownish-white; interior, whitish.

Measures up to 4 inches in length.

Papery Lantern Shell
(*Thracia papyracea*)

Conrad's Thracia
(*Thracia conradi*)

Convex Lantern Shell (*Thracia convexa*):
British Isles.
Occurs below lower shore, deep in muddy sand.
Shell thin, nearly rectangular; swollen; glossy; surface has wavy lines of granulations.
Exterior shell colour, pale yellowish-brown.
Measures up to $2\frac{1}{2}$ inches in length.

Papery Lantern Shell (*Thracia papyracea*):
Mediterranean coasts, but also ranges from north-west Africa to Atlantic coast of Europe and Iceland.
Occurs below lower shore, on muddy sand.
Shell almost convex; thin; a few concentric ridges; posterior truncated; large hinge ligament; half-circle shaped ossicle.
Exterior shell colour, white.
Measures up to an inch in length.

5 Univalves

ABALONES

The Abalones are large, sedentary molluscs which, like the
Limpets, live a similar existence clinging by the large, muscular
'foot' against rocks. They are vegetarian and feed on algae,
including the larger species, and their exterior shell may be
covered with marine growths and various marine creatures,
boring mussels, sponges, barnacles, piddocks, etc. The shell is a
very flat spiral, like an ear, shallow, curved, almost round, the
last whorl being large and prominent. It has a series of nearly-
round perforations – usually five – open, sometimes four or six,
near the outer margin. Through each of these projects a tube
filament from the mantle for sensory and respiratory purposes.
In young Abalones the first perforations are sealed with shell
material as the mollusc grows. The muscle flesh of the 'foot' of
these molluscs has been in high demand for many years in various
parts of the world as food, particularly in Asia, and this has
caused their decline. On the U.S.A. coasts they are now strictly
conserved by protective size and weight laws. Their rough
exterior shells, because of the beautiful, polished, iridescent,
nacreous interior, have also been much sought by makers of
jewellery and fancy articles. Sometimes the shell's interior
nacreous colour is not obvious if the mollusc has only recently
died, or until it has been polished. In the British Isles, Channel
Isles and Europe they are known as Ormers, Haliotis-shells,
Sea-Ears, or Ear-shells; in Australia as Mutton-Fish.

Black Abalone (*Haliotis cracherodi*):
Pacific coast U.S.A.; Mexico.
Occurs on lower shore and below.
Shell smooth, with up to 9 open perforations.
Exterior shell colour, bluish-black, blackish-grey; interior,

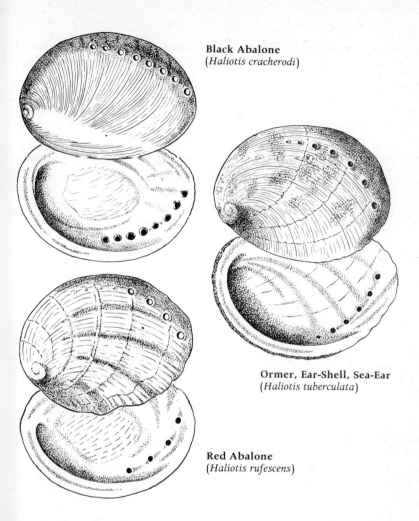

Black Abalone
(*Haliotis cracherodi*)

Ormer, Ear-Shell, Sea-Ear
(*Haliotis tuberculata*)

Red Abalone
(*Haliotis rufescens*)

whitish, iridescent.
Measures up to 7 inches in length.

Northern Green Abalone (*Haliotis walallensis*):
Pacific coast U.S.A. and Canada.
Occurs lower shore and below.
Shell elongated, flat with fine striae; up to 8 open perforations.
Exterior shell colour, red and bluish; interior, pearly-green.
Measures up to 4 inches in length.

Ormer, Ear-Shell, Sea-Ear (*Haliotis tuberculata*):
Channel Isles; Bay of Biscay, west coast France and Spain; Mediterranean.
Occurs on lower shore and below. Still extensively sought for food, but its 'foot' is tough and must be pounded to make it tender.
Exterior shell colour, dull reddish-brown.
Measures up to 4 inches long, Channel Isles; may be up to 6 inches Mediterranean.

Pink Abalone (*Haliotis corrugata*):
Pacific coast U.S.A.
Occurs on lower shore and below.
Shell irregularly corrugated; has a scalloped margin; up to 4 open perforations, each with a raised edge, volcano-like.
Exterior shell colour, brownish-pink; interior, iridescent pearly-pink.
Measures up to 7 inches in length.

Red Abalone (*Haliotis rufescens*):
Pacific coast U.S.A.
Occurs on lower shore and below.
Shell has irregular, lumpy surface; up to 4 open perforations.
Exterior shell colour, reddish-brown; interior, pearly; shell margin, reddish.
Measures up to 12 inches in length.

LIMPETS

The conical shape of their thick shell ensures that Limpets are quickly identifiable. They occur on rocks and stones, occasionally on other objects or large seaweeds, but not soft mud, sand, etc. The saying 'cling like a limpet', is very apt if one is describing anything with a very tight grip, for these molluscs certainly do so by means of their powerful muscular 'foot'. A clumsy approach makes Limpets grip tighter, so it is difficult to remove them when uncovered at low water without damaging the shells. More success is possible by waiting until they are covered by water; then a careful, sudden, sideways, surprise hit may remove an insecure specimen. Birds which prey on them, such as Oyster catchers, wrench them from the rocks when the Limpet has partly raised its shell prior to moving, respiring or feeding. In similar circumstances the collector, too, can carefully use a knife to prise one off. In rock pools they can be watched in swaying motion searching for algae and seaweed spores. To stay alive when exposed at low water they must retain some water around parts of their body. To do this the shell must be watertight and fit the uneven rock surface. Even seemingly smooth rocks are not completely flat and so, to fit its shell margin to an irregular rock, the Limpet either files the soft rock surface to make a deep groove or recess to exactly match its shell margin, or it may wear away the margin of its shell to align with the uneven hard rock surface. Examine one on a rock and you will see how perfectly it achieves a uniform effect, Having done this, they wander away in all directions from their own specially-made site on the rock to feed at high water but unerringly return to it and fit their shell securely into their own rock 'indentation' before low water or before the rock dries through exposure to air. Some rocks may have hundreds of these 'pit indentations' on their surface, made by many Limpet generations. Formerly, they were much gathered as food in Britain as they still are in other parts of the world. Empty shells are very common on the shore zones. Ranging over the world's coastlines there are several hundred species, all of which are vegetarian. Identification between certain species is not easy because they vary considerably and also hybridize with other species.

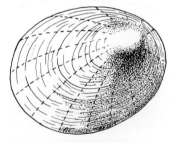

Blue-Rayed Limpet, Blue-Spotted Limpet, Kingfisher Limpet
(*Patina* [*Helcion*] *pellucida*)

Atlantic Plate Limpet (U.S.A.)
(*Acmaea testudinalis*),
Tortoiseshell Limpet (British Isles)
(*Acmaea* [*Patelloida*] *tessulata* [*testudinalis*])

113

Atlantic Plate Limpet (U.S.A.) (*Acmaea testudinalis*),
Tortoiseshell Limpet (British Isles) (*Acmaea* [*Patelloida*]
tessulata [*testudinalis*]):
Alaska; north-east coast U.S.A.; northern coast Canada; northern
and north-west coast British Isles; Isle of Man; east coast Ireland.
Occurs on lower shore and below.
Shell smooth-surfaced, with flattened cone, the apex close to
anterior margin.
Exterior shell colour, dull grey ground with mosaic-like, wavy,
irregular markings white and chestnut-brown or reddish-brown,
giving exterior resemblance to tortoiseshell; interior, variable,
white or pale blue with head-scar chocolate-brown.
Measures up to an inch in length in British Isles; $1\frac{1}{2}$ inches in
U.S.A.

**Blue-Rayed Limpet, Blue-Spotted Limpet, Kingfisher
Limpet** (*Patina* [*Helcion*] *pellucida*):
British Isles.
Occurs on lower shore and below, on oar-weed (Laminaria) and
other large seaweeds; young examples on fronds, old examples on
stems and holdfasts; may be washed ashore on oar-weed after
rough seas.
Shell smooth-surfaced, semi-transparent; flat cone with the apex
close to anterior margin.
Exterior shell colour, golden-brown or olive; young with a
varying number of lines of vivid blue spots radiating from the
apex to the margin, but blue lines or spots usually absent in the
thicker, old examples in order to be camouflaged on an excavated
stem or among a holdfast; interior, shade of blue.
Measures up to an inch in length.

China Limpet (*Patella aspera*):
British Isles.
Occurs on exposed lower shore, occasionally in weedy rock pools
on middle and upper shore zones.
Shell rough-surfaced, sharply-ribbed, more oblong and flattened
than Common Limpet, with apex close to anterior margin; margin
crenated. Has orange 'foot', Common Limpet's 'foot' being
greyish.

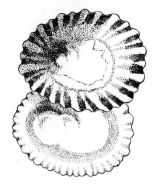

China Limpet (*Patella aspera*)

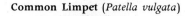

Common Limpet (*Patella vulgata*)

Giant Owl Limpet (*Lottia gigantea*)

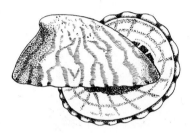

Fingered Limpet (*Acmaea digitalis*)

Exterior shell colour, variable, as Common Limpet, but interior smooth, porcellaneous white, with pale orange or cream head-scar.

Measures up to 2 inches in length.

Common Limpet (*Patella vulgata*):
British Isles.
Occurs on upper, middle and lower shore zones.
Shell thick, tall, conical, rough-surfaced; ribbed from apex to margin; margin crenated; apex not curved. 'Foot' greyish. Old specimens' exterior may be worn smooth.
Exterior shell colour, variable, plain greenish, brownish, olive-grey or yellowish, with some purple rays; interior, white or yellow, glossy, surface colour showing through, with a white varying to brown, not orange, head-scar.
Measures up to $2\frac{1}{2}$ inches in length.

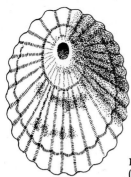

Lister's Keyhole Limpet
(*Diodora listeri*)

Keyhole Limpet
(*Diodora [Fissurella] apertura*)

Fingered Limpet (*Acmaea digitalis*):
Alaska; Pacific coast Canada and U.S.A.
Occurs on lower shore.
Shell elliptical; anterior end narrower; has a hooked apex; very weak, irregular, radial ribs almost flat; margin slightly waved.
Exterior shell colour, grey, with an irregular pattern of black streaks and white mottling.
Measures up to an inch in length.

Giant Owl Limpet (*Lottia gigantea*):
Pacific coast U.S.A.; Mexico.
Occurs on lower shore.
Shell oval; apex close to anterior margin; numerous low radiating ribs.
Exterior shell colour, yellowish-white and brown; interior, wide glossy brown margin, centre and apex bluish-white and sometimes brown.
Measures up to 4 inches in length.

Great Keyhole Limpet (*Megathura crenulata*):
Pacific coast U.S.A.
Occurs on lower shore.
Shell broadly oval, smooth-surfaced; finely-ribbed, with a large, oval, apical opening or 'keyhole'.
Exterior shell colour, brown or mauvish; apical opening white-bordered.
Measures up to 6 inches in length; the largest U.S. limpet.

116

Keyhole Limpet (*Diodora* [*Fissurella*] *apertura*):
British Isles.
Occurs on lower shore and below.
Shell strongly radially-ribbed from apex to margin; with a single apical 'keyhole' opening, used as part of the respiratory and waste expulsion system.
Exterior shell colour, yellowish-white with one or more broad, darker reddish or greenish-brown rays.
Measures up to $1\frac{1}{2}$ inches in length.

Linné's Puncturella (*Puncturella noachina*):
Alaska; northern and east coast Canada, north-east coast U.S.A.; Scandinavia, northern Europe.
Occurs on lower shore and below, *under* rocks.
Shell elongated, compressed laterally; margin crenulated; up to 26 narrow ribs; has a tiny slit in front of apex.
Exterior shell colour, brownish-grey or pale brownish-white.
Measures up to $\frac{1}{2}$-inch in length.

Lister's Keyhole Limpet (*Diodora listeri*):
South-east coast U.S.A.; West Indies.
Occurs on lower shore.
Shell strongly radially-ribbed and ridged from apex to margin; margin crenated; ribs usually alternately large and small; a single 'keyhole' apical opening with a callus encircling interior of 'keyhole'.
Exterior shell colour, white, cream or greyish; interior, whitish-grey.
Measures up to 2 inches in length.

Patella Intermedia (*Depressa*):
South-west coast England; Channel Isles.
Occurs on exposed lower shore, occasionally in weedy rock pools on upper shore and middle shore zones.
Shell rough-surfaced, ribbed, more oval and flatter than Common Limpet; margin crenated; 'foot' dark grey or black.
Exterior shell colour, variable, as Common Limpet, but apex crown orange and has dark ray areas on exterior margin; interior, dark colour with central golden-yellow, orange or cream head-scar and rayed to the margin.
Measures up to $1\frac{1}{2}$ inches in length.

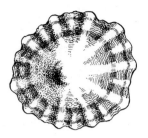
Patella Intermedia (*Depressa*)

Slit Limpet (*Emarginula reticulata*)

Volcano Limpet (*Fissurella volcano*)

White Tortoiseshell Limpet (*Acmaea virginea*)

Rough Limpet (*Acmaea scabra*):
Pacific coast Canada and U.S.A.; Mexico.
Occurs lower shore and below.
Shell elliptical; prominently ribbed, with up to 25 ribs; flat cone with the apex close to the anterior margin; margin crenated.
Exterior shell colour, greyish-white; interior dull white.
Measures up to $1\frac{1}{2}$ inches in length.

Slit Limpet (*Emarginula reticulata*):
British Isles.
Occurs on lower shore and below.
Shell identified by vertical slit or marginal notch on anterior edge used as part of the respiratory system; ribbed and cross-lined from apex to margin, the radial ribs being narrow but the crossing-ribs are narrower; apex distinctly curved.
Exterior shell colour, variable, usually white, grey or brownish.
Measures up to $\frac{1}{2}$-inch in length.

Volcano Limpet (*Fissurella volcano*):
Pacific coast U.S.A.
Occurs on lower shore.
Shell has a few, almost flat, wide radial ribs; 'keyhole' apical

opening sited fractionally closer to narrower anterior margin; 'keyhole' has a callus.
Exterior shell colour, brownish-grey with darker or mauvish ray markings; interior white; callus surrounded by a pink line.
Measures up to an inch in length.

White Tortoiseshell Limpet (*Acmaea virginea*):
British Isles; Channel Isles.
Occurs on lower shore and below, among stones, shells, also on oar-weed (*Laminaria*).
Shell similar to Tortoiseshell Limpet; smooth-surfaced; with flattened cone, the apex close to anterior margin.
Exterior shell colour, dull white or pinkish with white, pink or brownish ray markings.
Measures up to $\frac{3}{4}$-inch in length.

TOP SHELLS

In shape they are wide at the base, either rounded or conical, though some species have a depressed appearance. The aperture is rounded, closed by a limy or horny 'lid' or operculum, which is sometimes spirally patterned. They may have been called Top Shells because of a similarity in shape to children's whipping tops. Due to their having a primitive respiratory system and being killed quickly by sandy, muddy or polluted water, they frequent only clean water, on rocks, stones and seaweeds, not on mud. Empty shells are cast up on higher shore zones. If worn by movement against another surface the beautiful nacreous layer beneath the shell surface is revealed. All Top Shell molluscs are vegetarian.

Calliostoma Papillosum:
Channel Isles; west and north-west England; Wales.
Occurs below lower shore.
Shell straight-sided pyramid; flat base; 10 whorls; has up to 8 concentric ridges with other minor ridges; a sharply-pointed cone.
Exterior shell colour, whitish-yellow with red-brown markings.
Measures up to $1\frac{1}{2}$ inches in height, slightly less wide.

Calliostoma Papillosum

Channelled Top Shell
(*Calliostoma canaliculatum*)

Cantharidus Exaspertus:
Channel Isles; south-west coast England.
Occurs lower shore and below.
Shell straight-sided; flattened base; up to 8 whorls, each with up to 5 spiral ridges; sharply-pointed apex cone.
Exterior shell colour, pink or red, may have broken pattern of spots; apex pink or red.
Measures up to $\frac{1}{2}$-inch in height, slightly less wide.

Channelled Top Shell (*Calliostoma canaliculatum*):
Alaska; Pacific coast Canada and U.S.A.
Occurs on lower shore and below.
Shell straight-sided pyramid; flattened base; up to 5 whorls, each with up to 9 prominent spiral ridges between sutures; a sharply-pointed apex cone.
Exterior shell colour, creamy-yellowish or brownish.
Measures up to $1\frac{1}{2}$ inches in height.

Flat or Purple Top Shell (*Gibbula umbilicalis*):
South-west coast England; west coast Scotland; Ireland; Isle of Man.
Occurs on middle shore and lower shore.
Shell depressed, not pointed pyramid shape; flat based, round umbilicus; up to 7 whorls; deep sutures; blunt apex.
Exterior shell colour, greenish ground with oblique, wide, red or purplish stripes or zig-zags, with green and orange on the outer lip.
Measures up to $\frac{3}{4}$-inch in height, slightly more wide.

Gibbula Magus:
South-west and west coast England; Wales; west coast Scotland; Orkney and Shetland Isles; Ireland.
Occurs on lower shore and below.
Shell depressed, not pointed pyramid shape; flat base, with a prominent keel or ridge around base; wide umbilicus; up to 8 whorls irregularly ridged and knobbed; deep sutures; blunt apex.
Exterior shell colour, yellowish-white with pink, reddish or purple oblique streaks and markings.
Measures up to an inch in height, $1\frac{1}{4}$ inches wide.

Gibbula Pennanti:
Channel Isles.
Occurs middle shore and lower shore.
Shell shape similar to Flat or Purple Top Shell, but adult is less angular and smaller, also imperforate.
Exterior shell colour, greenish or greyish ground with clear purple oblique stripes.
Measures up to $\frac{1}{2}$-inch in height, slightly more wide.

Greenland Top Shell (British Isles), Greenland Margarite (U.S.A.) (*Margarites groenlandicus*):
North and east coast Canada; north-east coast U.S.A.; west coast Scotland; Orkney and Shetland Isles.
Occurs on lower shore and below.
Shell thin, smooth, globular; up to 6 rotund whorls; upper surface with fine striae and puckering beneath the deep suture; narrow, deep umbilicus.
Exterior shell colour, plain creamy-brown, rosy-brown or flesh.
Measures up to $\frac{1}{2}$-inch in height, same width.

Grey Top Shell, 'Silver Tommy' (*Gibbula cineraria*):
British Isles.
Occurs on middle shore and lower shore.
Shell depressed, not pointed pyramid shape; flattened shape and appearance varying among examples depending on the habitat; more depressed if on Laminaria than on rocks; usually not so flat as the Flat or Purple Top Shell; up to 7 whorls, upper whorls rounded, lower whorls flattened; blunt-keeled base; small,

Flat or Purple Top Shell
(*Gibbula umbilicalis*)

Gibbula Magus

Grey Top Shell, 'Silver Tommy'
(*Gibbula cineraria*)

Greenland Top Shell (British Isles), Greenland Margarite (U.S.A.) (*Margarites groenlandicus*)

Grooved Top Shell
(*Cantharidus striatus*)

narrow umbilicus; blunt apex.
Exterior shell colour, dull pale grey or yellowish ground with narrow, close, oblique dark purple-brown or dark grey streaks. Nickname given due to colour of nacreous layer revealed when grey shell surface is worn off.
Measures up to $\frac{3}{4}$-inch in height and width.

Gibbula Variegata is a smaller variety of *G. cineraria*, occurs on the Channel Isles, French and Mediterranean coasts, the chief difference being that in addition to a grey ground and dark purple stripes, it has wide ray markings of dark reddish-brown on the upper part of the whorls.

Grooved Top Shell (*Cantharidus striatus*):
South-west coast England; south coast Ireland; Channel Isles. Occurs on lower shore, but usually only where eel-grass (*Zostera*)

is present.

Shell straight-sided; base narrow in proportion to height; up to 8 whorls, the last 3 whorls each having up to 9 spiral ridges with tiny striae between the ridges; sharply-pointed apex.

Exterior shell colour, white, with black, red, or brown oblique streaks.

Measures up to $\frac{1}{2}$-inch in height, slightly less wide.

Painted Top Shell, Common Top Shell (*Calliostoma zizyphinum*):

British Isles.

Occurs on lower shore and below.

Shell straight-sided pyramid; near-flat base; up to 12 variably and finely ridged, flattened whorls; sharply pointed cone; no umbilicus; horny operculum has numerous whorls. Variable in shape and some authorities have named these as varieties, but general appearance makes the Painted Top Shell an unmistakably beautiful species.

Exterior shell colour, flesh-pink, purplish-pink or pale yellow ground with red-brown streaks or purple-spotted white bands; *C. zizyphinum var.* **Lyonsi** is an entirely white variety. Apex may be pearly if worn.

Measures up to $1\frac{1}{4}$ inches in height and slightly less in width.

Ribbed Top Shell (*Calliostoma ligatum*):

Alaska; Pacific coast Canada and U.S.A.

Occurs on lower shore, among stones and seaweed.

Shell thick, pyramidal, whorls rounded, with spiral ridges; sharply pointed apex.

Exterior shell colour, dark brown, with ridges tan coloured; aperture pearly-white.

Measures up to an inch in height, same in width.

Speckled Tegula Top Shell (*Tegula gallina*):

Pacific coast U.S.A.

Occurs on lower shore and below.

Shell thick, heavy, more upright than rounded; up to 6 whorls, top whorls usually worn away to reveal nacreous layer; umbilicus closed.

Exterior shell colour, greyish-greenish or darker, with numerous

Speckled Tegula Top Shell
(*Tegula gallina*)

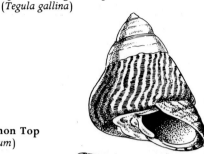

Painted Top Shell, Common Top Shell (*Calliostoma zizyphinum*)

Thick Top Shell, Toothed Winkle
(*Gibbula [Monodonta] lineata*)

West Indian Top Shell
(*Cittarium pica*)

narrow zig-zag white stripes.
Measures up to 1½ inches in height.

Thick Top Shell, Toothed Winkle (*Gibbula [Monodonta] lineata*):
South-west coast England to North Wales; Ireland; Channel Isles.
Occurs on middle shore, on rocks.
Shell thick, more rounded, conical; up to 6 whorls; blunt apex; large mother-of-pearl aperture oval, the very thick, broad, inner lip having a single, strong, tubercular knob or 'tooth' in its middle; large, shallow umbilicus partially hidden by the inner lip. Exterior shell colour, dull greyish, greenish, or yellowish ground, with dark purple, almost black, wavy, zig-zag streaks; the blunt apex is usually eroded on adult shells to reveal yellow.
Measures up to an inch in height, same in width.

West Indian Top Shell (*Cittarium pica*):
South-east coast U.S.A.; West Indies.
Occurs on lower shore, among rocks.
Shell thick, heavy; rough-surfaced; flattened base; up to 4 rounded whorls; deep umbilicus; circular operculum horny.
Exterior shell colour, purple-black, with numerous whitish mottled areas; aperture interior, pearly-white; operculum green-blue in living specimens, brown after death.
Measures up to 3 inches in height, slightly wider.

The Turban Shells have thick, heavy shells, with a hard, limy operculum and resemble the Periwinkles and Top Shells. They are mainly tropical, occurring in shallow water, feeding on algae.

Chestnut Turban (*Turbo castanea*):
South-east coast U.S.A.; Mexico; Central America; Brazil; West Indies.
Occurs on lower shore and below.
Shell thick, conical; up to 6 beaded, rounded whorls, rounded body whorl largest; resembles an elongated Periwinkle; pointed apex; large aperture rounded.
Exterior shell colour, chestnut-brown, dark brown, smaller whorls may be paler; inner lip and aperture white.
Measures up to $1\frac{1}{2}$ inches in height.

Green Turban (*Turbo marmoratus*):
Indonesia; Australia.
Occurs on lower shore and below.
Shell thick, heavy, conical; up to 6 rounded whorls, body whorl largest, with small knobs on shoulder; pointed apex; aperture large, rounded.
Exterior shell colour, green, with brown and white bands; inner lip and aperture white.
Measures up to 8 inches in height.

Gold-mouthed Turban (*Turbo chrysostomus*):
Indo-Pacific.

Occurs on coral reefs.

Shell thick, heavy; up to 6 whorls, sides of whorls straight, tops of whorls semi-flattened – making clear definition between whorls; body whorl largest with small knobs on shoulders; prominent spiral ridges; pointed apex; large aperture rounded. Exterior shell colour, white, greenish, pale brown, with darker brown band markings; inner lip and margin of aperture white; aperture orange-gold, glossy, or whitish.

Measures up to 3 inches in height.

NERITE SHELLS

The Nerite molluscs have rounded shells with a large body whorl and slightly resemble the Periwinkles. They are tough and chiefly found on rocks and may occur in large numbers. The identifying feature is the inner lip which has a varying number of projections or 'teeth', although in some instances these may be very minute or absent. The operculum is limy and may bear pimples and it also has a small projection used for muscular attachment. All Nerite molluscs are vegetarian.

Four-Toothed Nerite
(*Nerita versicolor*)

Bleeding Tooth Nerite
(*Nerita peloronta*)

Bleeding Tooth Nerite (*Nerita peloronta*):

South-east coast U.S.A.; Caribbean.

Occurs on lower and middle shore, on rocks.

Shell rounded, large body whorl; large aperture and outer and inner lip bearing two projections or 'teeth'.

Exterior shell colour, brownish-white, with dark brown, almost black, streak markings; outer and inner lip, white, except for reddish-orange blotch surrounding two white 'teeth'.

Measures up to 2 inches in height.

Four-Toothed Nerite (*Nerita versicolor*):
South-east coast U.S.A.
Occurs on lower shore, on rocks.
Shell rounded, large body whorl; large aperture and outer and inner lip, the inner lip bearing four prominent projections or 'teeth'.
Exterior shell colour, dull white, with black and reddish streak markings, outer and inner lip white; four 'teeth' on inner lip white; operculum, greyish-brown with pimples.
Measures up to $\frac{3}{4}$-inch in height.

PERIWINKLES AND CHINK SHELLS (British Isles) OR LACUNA PERIWINKLES (U.S.A.)

The Periwinkles are among the most familiar and common sea shells. They are solidly tough and rounded and thus able to resist and endure the wave action on their rock, stone and similar shore habitat and survive being knocked off and rolled along the shore. Unlike the Top Shells, when eroded they do not show a pearly nacreous layer. The shell has no umbilicus, the columella being smooth, while the ear-shaped operculum is thick and horny. The Edible Periwinkle is a popular item of sea food in Britain and Europe, but less so in the U.S.A. At low water live periwinkles revealed by the receding tide can be found dormant in breakwater crevices, undersides of rocks, seaweeds and other shore objects, anywhere where there is moisture, awaiting the return of the tide.

   The similar, smaller Chink Shells or Lacuna Periwinkles can be identified from the Periwinkles by a long groove or slit on the columella or pillar, from which they derive their name; they have a chinklike umbilicus; also the shell is less thick and tough.

Checkered Periwinkle (*Littorina scutulata*):
Alaska; Pacific coast Canada and U.S.A.
Occurs on the lower shore, on seaweed.
Shell thick, more slender, upright and smoother; up to 5 whorls; has a clearly pointed cone.
Exterior shell colour, dark red-brown, with bluish or whitish irregular, wavy, spiral band markings; aperture, pale brown.
Measures up to $\frac{1}{2}$-inch in height.

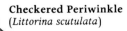
Checkered Periwinkle
(*Littorina scutulata*)

Common Edible Periwinkle (British Isles), European Periwinkle (U.S.A.) (*Littorina littorea*)

Eroded Periwinkle
(*Littorina planaxis*)

Flat Periwinkle (British Isles)
(*Littorina littoralis* [*obtusata*]),
Northern Yellow Periwinkle
(**U.S.A.**) (*Littorina obtusata*)

Common Edible Periwinkle (British Isles), European Periwinkle (U.S.A.) (*Littorina littorea*):
British Isles; Europe; Atlantic coast Canada; north-east coast U.S.A.
Occurs on middle shore and lower shore, on rocks, stones, chalk boulders, among seaweed and other objects.
Shell rounded; up to 8 whorls, with sculptured surface; only slightly sutured; sharply-pointed spire.
Exterior shell colour, variable, dark grey, black, brown, olive or reddish, with darker concentric lines.
Measures up to an inch in height.

Eroded Periwinkle (*Littorina planaxis*):
Pacific coast U.S.A.
Occurs on middle shore and lower shore, on rocks.
Shell rounded, smooth; up to 4 whorls; body whorl has a flat eroded area beside the white columella; outer lip thin.
Exterior shell colour, greyish-brown, with greyish-whitish spots and markings and darker wavy markings.
Measures up to $\frac{1}{2}$-inch in height.

Flat Periwinkle (British Isles) (*Littorina littoralis* [*obtusata*]),
Northern Yellow Periwinkle (U.S.A.) (*Littorina obtusata*):
British Isles; north and east coast Canada; north-east coast
U.S.A.
Occurs on middle shore and lower shore, on wrack (Fucus) and
other seaweeds.
Shell rounded; smooth; up to 5 whorls, but the first 4 are small
and insignificant so that last or body whorl comprises almost the
entire shell; flattened apex; large aperture.
Exterior shell colour, variable, uniform brown, red, purple,
orange, yellow, green, occasionally white, or streaked or banded
with one of these colours.
Measures up to $\frac{1}{2}$-inch in height, slightly wider.

**Rough Periwinkle (British Isles), Northern Rough
Periwinkle (U.S.A.)** (*Littorina saxatilis*):
British Isles; north and east coast Canada; north-east U.S.A.;
Alaska; Pacific coast Canada; north-west coast U.S.A.
Occurs on upper shore and top of middle shore, on rocks.
Shell rounded; up to 9 whorls; spiral, flattened ribs; deep sutures;
clearly pointed apex. Shell surface feels rough to the finger touch.
Exterior shell colour very variable, blackish, grey, brown,
purple, red, orange, yellow, white, often spiral-banded in a
different tint or may have mosaic pattern.
Measures up to $\frac{3}{4}$-inch in height, $\frac{1}{2}$-inch wide.

Small Periwinkle (*Littorina neritoides*):
British Isles.
Occurs on upper shore and above high-water level in splash zone,
in protecting crevices, in rocks, cliff faces, in semi-stagnant pools;
preferring more exposed habitats, particularly those facing
south, than other Periwinkle species; sometimes nearly on dry
land or sites only infrequently wetted by spray. Has a 'lung' to
obtain oxygen from air. May be in a transitional stage of becoming a land mollusc.
Shell fragile, smooth, long conical; up to 6 whorls; body whorl
comprises two-thirds of entire shell; pointed apex.
Exterior shell colour, dark brown, brownish-grey; may have
pale brown or yellowish at base; has a 'bloom' on the surface

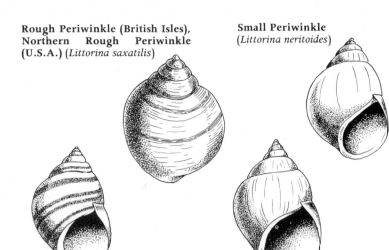

Rough Periwinkle (British Isles), Northern Rough Periwinkle (U.S.A.) (*Littorina saxatilis*)

Small Periwinkle (*Littorina neritoides*)

Banded Chink Shell (British Isles), Northern Lacuna (U.S.A.) (*Lucuna vincta*)

Thick Chink Shell (*Lacuna crassior*)

similar to that on plums, grapes, etc.

Measures up to $\frac{1}{4}$-inch in height, less wide; Smallest British Periwinkle.

Banded Chink Shell (British Isles), Northern Lacuna (U.S.A.) (*Lacuna vincta*):

British Isles; North and east coast Canada; north-east coast U.S.A.; Pacific coast Canada and U.S.A.

Occurs on lower shore and below, on rocks, stones, seaweeds, especially oarweed (*Laminaria*).

Shell thin, smooth surface semi-transparent; long conical, not turreted; up to 5 rounded whorls, last or body whorl comprising half of entire shell; sharply pointed apex; thin periostracum.

Exterior shell colour, glossy pale yellow, buff-yellow, pale brown, with up to 4 paler bands.

Measures up to $\frac{1}{2}$-inch in height.

Thick Chink Shell (*Lacuna crassior*):

British Isles.

Occurs on lower shore and below, particularly on rocks and

stones in sandy areas, but it also occurs above high-water level exposed to the air.

Shell thicker than L. vincta; turreted; up to 7 whorls; with deep suture; thick periostracum forms irregular folds; blunt apex; lip expanded and thin; groove or slit on the columella or pillar may not be present.

Exterior shell colour, yellow, brownish-yellow.

Measures up to $\frac{3}{4}$-inch in height, $\frac{1}{2}$ inch wide.

The Sundial Shells are a small family, there being forty species, all living in tropical regions. Some have a widely coiled shell, the umbilicus being open to its apex. The operculum is horny. Also known as Staircase Shells because the spiralling resembles a winding staircase.

Common Atlantic Sundial Shell (*Architectonica nobilis*):
South-east coast U.S.A.; Caribbean; West Indies; west coast Mexico, Central America, Colombia, Ecuador, Peru.

Occurs on lower shore, on sand.

Shell compressed, with up to 5 beaded, spiral coils; deep umbilicus bordered by spiral beading; aperture irregular-oval.

Exterior shell colour, above view, pale brown with darker brown spiral bead narkings, below view, pale brown with a few brown bead markings; aperture white.

Measures up to $1\frac{1}{2}$ inches in diameter.

Staircase Shell, Sundial Shell (*Architectonica perspectiva*):
Indo-Pacific.

Occurs on lower shore and below.

Shell compressed, with up to 5 beaded spiral coils; deep umbilicus bordered by spiral beading; aperture irregular-oval.

Exterior shell colour, above view, pale brown with dark brown, yellow-brown and white continuous spirals; some spirals broken into yellow-brown and dark brown broken spots, below view, pale grey and white, with broken spirals of yellow-brown and dark brown spots; umbilicus spiral beading brown; aperture brown and grey.

Measures up to $1\frac{1}{2}$ inches in diameter.

SLIPPER LIMPETS (British Isles) AND BONNET LIMPETS (British Isles), CAP SHELLS AND CUP-AND-SAUCER SHELLS (U.S.A.)

The Slipper Limpets, known as Slipper Shells or Boat Shells in the U.S.A., are Mesogastropod Limpets, which live a permanent mode of life like the more familiar Archaeogastropod Limpets described earlier in this chapter. They have an obvious horizontal interior ledge or platform, a modified columella, like a deck of a ship, which gave rise to one American name, but this ledge also gives the shell a resemblance to a rounded slipper, hence the English name. More accurately, it could be said to be scoop-like.

Related to them by also being in the Mesogastropod family are the Bonnet Limpets or Cap Shells and Cup-and-Saucer Shells, some of which have a curved apex or a 'cup' ledge on their interior.

Bonnet Limpet, Fool's Cap, Cap of Liberty, Hungarian Cap (*Capulus ungaricus*)

American Slipper Limpet (British Isles), Atlantic Slipper Shell (U.S.A.) (*Crepidula fornicata*)

American Slipper Limpet (British Isles), Atlantic Slipper Shell (U.S.A.) (*Crepidula fornicata*):

East, south, south-west coast England; south Wales; south-west Ireland; North Sea coast Europe, including Holland; Atlantic coast Canada and U.S.A.; Gulf of Mexico. Accidentally introduced into England from North America with American oysters laid to restock depleted Native Oyster beds in the 1880s.

Occurs on lower shore and below; a serious pest in oyster beds; in large numbers causes silting and their weight smothers the oysters to which they are attached, or they starve them of plankton food.

Shell oval, but shape variable, flat or taller and curving; with several growth lines; interior ledge horizontal. May consist of a chain of up to 12 individual molluscs, one attached to the back of the other.

Exterior shell colour, dull white, brownish-white, creamy-pink, streaked with pink or brown; interior, pearly pink and brown blotches on interior margin; platform or ledge, buff.

Measures up to $1\frac{1}{2}$ inches in length, British Isles; up to 2 inches, U.S.A.

Bonnet Limpet, Fool's Cap, Cap of Liberty, Hungarian Cap (*Capulus ungaricus*):

British Isles.

Occurs on lower shore and below, on rocks, stones and shells, also in oyster beds and on scallops.

Shell ovate, obviously curved to apex; prominent, irregular, concentric growth lines; the beak or apex curves down.

Exterior shell colour, variable, whitish-yellow to reddish-brown, but may be obscured by dirty brown, coarse, horny periostracum, which also covers the radiating ribs, but worn off the apex; interior, white or pink.

Measures up to $1\frac{3}{4}$ inches in diameter.

Californian Cap Shell (*Capulus californicus*):

Pacific coast U.S.A. and Mexico.

Occurs on lower shore and below, on valves of the San Diego Scallop.

Shell thin; irregularly-ovate, similar to Bonnet Limpet; curved to apex, the small apex hooked downwards; numerous prominent, irregular, concentric growth lines.

Exterior shell colour, whitish; periostracum, pale brown; interior, white with yellowish, horseshoe-shaped muscle scar.

Measures up to an inch in diameter.

Chinaman's Hat, Cup-and-Saucer Limpet (*Calyptraea chinensis*):

South-west coast England; Channel Isles; France.

Occurs on lower shore, attached on stones and shells; smaller males may be found attached on shell of larger female.

Shell thin, round, conical, sometimes almost flat, with a central

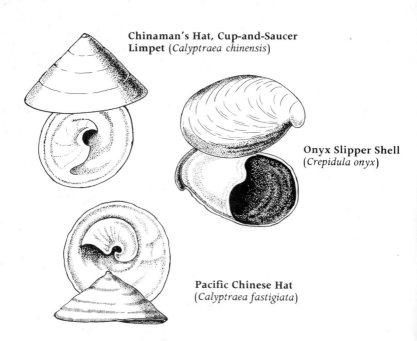

Chinaman's Hat, Cup-and-Saucer Limpet (*Calyptraea chinensis*)

Onyx Slipper Shell (*Crepidula onyx*)

Pacific Chinese Hat (*Calyptraea fastigiata*)

raised nipple-like beak or apex; spiral growth lines; interior has a conspicuous oblique ledge or plate on posterior half.
Exterior shell colour, pinkish.
Measures up to an inch in diameter.

Onyx Slipper Shell (*Crepidula onyx*):
Pacific coast U.S.A., Central America and South America.
Occurs on lower shore and below, on rocks, also as chains upon each other.
Shell oval, with several growth lines; interior platform or ledge thin with a wavy edge.
Exterior shell colour, pale brown; interior, glossy brown-red; platform, pearly-white.
Measures up to 2 inches in length.

Pacific Chinese Hat (*Calyptraea fastigiata*):
Alaska; Pacific coast Canada and U.S.A.
Occurs on lower shore and below.
Shell round, conical, with a central, raised, nipple-like apex;

smooth, spiral growth lines; interior has a twisted ledge or 'cup'.
Exterior shell colour, white; thin periostracum, pale yellow;
interior, glossy white.
Measures up to an inch in diameter.

Spiny Slipper Shell (*Crepidula aculeata*):
South-east coast U.S.A.; West Indies.
Occurs on lower shore, on rocks.
Shell irregular-oval, with a curving beak or apex; rough exterior
has numerous spines; interior platform or ledge has a raised
central ridge.
Exterior shell colour, white, pinkish-brown or orange-brown;
interior, brownish; platform, white.
Measures up to an inch in length.

Striate Cup-and-Saucer Shell (*Crucibulum striatum*):
East coast Canada and U.S.A.
Occurs on lower shore and below, on rocks.
Shell round, conical; with apex curved, twisted off-centre;
numerous small radiating ridges; interior has twisted 'cup'.
Exterior shell colour, brownish; interior, glossy yellowish-
brown; 'cup' ledge, white.
Measures up to an inch in diameter.

Western White Slipper Shell (*Crepidula nummaria*):
South coast Alaska; Pacific coast U.S.A., Central America.
Occurs on lower shore, on rocks and shells.
Shell shape variable, oval, usually concave, with prominent
growth lines; interior platform or ledge has a raised ridge.
Exterior shell colour, white; thin periostracum, tan; interior,
white.
Measures up to an inch in length.

COWRIES AND TRIVIAS

Cowries begin as spiral shells but as they develop so the large
body whorl grows over and encloses the previously formed
whorls, until the mature Cowrie has no trace of the spiral whorls
and takes the well-known shape. The aperture has become a
longitudinal slit almost the full length of the under-surface, with

'teeth' on each side, and is not closed with an operculum. Some of the exotic, colourful, tropical species are large, heavy and thick due to the living mollusc's lobed mantle tissues, which extend over much of the shell, continually adding lining material to the shell. Instead of a horny periostracum the exterior shell is coated with hard, smooth, glossy material to protect the mantle from friction.

The Trivias resemble miniature Cowries and are included here for this reason, but belong to a different family.

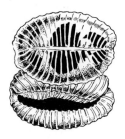

Atlantic Coffee Bean Trivia
(*Trivia pediculus*)

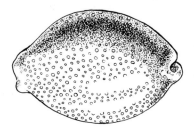

Atlantic Deer Cowrie
(*Cypraea cervus*)

Atlantic Coffee Bean Trivia (*Trivia pediculus*):
South-east coast U.S.A.; West Indies.
Occurs on lower shore and below, on coral.
Shell oval; up to 19 prominent ribs on outer lip.
Exterior shell colour, upper surface, yellowish-brown or pink-brown with 6 darker brown irregular spots or blotches; under-surface, yellow-brown or pink-brown.
Measures up to $\frac{1}{2}$-inch in length.

Atlantic Deer Cowrie (*Cypraea cervus*):
South-east coast U.S.A.; Gulf of Mexico; West Indies.
Occurs on lower shore and below.
Shell oval, similar to Measled Cowrie, but larger, with smaller spots.
Exterior shell colour, medium to dark brown, with plain, small, whitish spots, the latter not having brown centres as in Measled Cowrie; aperture 'teeth', brown.
Measures up to 7 inches in length.

Californian Trivia
(*Trivia californiana*)

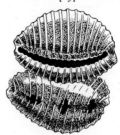

European Cowrie, Spotted Cowrie,
Nun, John O'Groats, Grottie-
Buckie, Stick-Farthing
(*Trivia monacha* [*Cypraea europaea*])

Atlantic Grey Cowrie (*Cypraea cinerea*):
South-east coast U.S.A.; Gulf of Mexico; Caribbean.
Occurs below lower shore, among coral.
Shell oval or pear-shaped; numerous 'teeth' on aperture margin.
Exterior shell colour, upper surface, purplish-red or brownish-mauve; sides with darker brown spots and flecks; under-surface, creamy-white, with mauvish-brown between the 'teeth'.
Measures up to an inch in length.

Californian Trivia (*Trivia californiana*):
Pacific coast U.S.A.; Mexico.
Occurs on lower shore and below.
Shell oval; up to 15 ribs.
Exterior shell colour, upper surface, mauvish-brown with a white area on centre; under-surface, mauvish-brown.
Measures up to $\frac{1}{2}$-inch in length.

Chestnut Cowrie (*Cypraea spadicea*):
South-west Pacific coast U.S.A.
Occurs on lower shore and below, among rocks.
Shell pear-shaped; aperture narrow, with up to 25 'teeth' on each side of it.
Exterior shell colour, upper surface, chestnut-brown, with a darker, brownish-black band and white encircling margin; under-surface, white; 'teeth', white.
Measures up to 2 inches in length.

European Cowrie, Spotted Cowrie, Nun, John O' Groats, Grottie-Buckie, Stick-Farthing (*Trivia monacha* [*Cypraea europaea*]):
British Isles; Channel Isles; Europe.
Occurs on lower shore and below, usually rocks, feeding on Sea Squirts. Empty shells sometimes extremely numerous on shore.
Shell oval; up to 25 ribs.
Exterior shell colour, white, with three purple-brown spots on upper surface.
Measures up to $\frac{1}{2}$-inch in length.

Hump-Back Cowrie (*Cypraea mauritiana*):
Indonesia; South-east Asia; Pacific islands.
Occurs in deep water below lower shore.
Shell oval, but with distinct raised area on upper surface giving hump-backed appearance.
Exterior shell colour, upper surface, dark brown with numerous whitish-brown spots, some joined; under-surface, dark brown, paler near aperture, whitish-brown edge to aperture; 'teeth', brown.
Measures up to 3 inches in length.

Lurid Cowrie (*Cypraea lurida*):
Mediterranean.
Occurs below lower shore.
Shell oval.
Exterior shell colour, upper surface, greyish-brown, each end having orange-buff area with two dark almost black spots; under-surface, white; 'teeth' white.
Measures up to $1\frac{1}{2}$ inches in length.

Measled Cowrie (*Cypraea zebra*):
South-east coast U.S.A.; Gulf of Mexico; Central America; Brazil.
Occurs on lower shore, among or near rocks.
Shell oval.
Exterior shell colour, upper surface, dark brown, with numerous small whitish spots, some of these having brown centres; under-surface, dark brown, with yellowish-brown margin to aperture; 'teeth', brown.
Measures up to 3 inches in length.

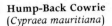
Hump-Back Cowrie
(*Cypraea mauritiana*)

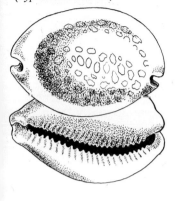

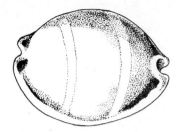

Lurid Cowrie (*Cypraea lurida*)

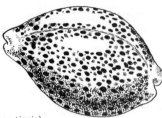

Tiger Cowrie (*Cypraea tigris*)

Tiger Cowrie (*Cypraea tigris*):
South-east Asia.
Occurs below lower shore.
Shell oval-rounded; large, wide aperture.
Exterior shell colour, upper surface, brownish-white and greyish-blue with numerous variably-sized, medium-brown and dark brown spots and blotches; may be a paler area down the centre of the upper surface, linking one side of the aperture to the other; under-surface, white and bluish, may have brownish markings on interior of lip; 'teeth' white.
Measures up to 4 inches in length.

Unspotted European Cowrie (*Trivia arctica*):
British Isles.
Occurs on lower shore and below; empty shells occasionally on shore.
Shell similar to relative European Cowrie (*T. monacha*), but slightly smaller and has no spots on upper surface.
Measures up to ½-inch in length.

SHELLS WITH TALL SPIRES

There are a considerable number of Gastropod molluscs, with shells shaped with an elongated cone, which can be found either alive, sometimes living in abundant colonies, or as empty shells cast up on the shore. I have combined some of these so that the collector will have details of them readily available to make identification easier, but they are members of several groups and though listed together are not necessarily closely related.

Bittium Simplex:
Channel Isles.
Occurs on lower shore.
Shell similar to Needle Whelk (*B. reticulatum*) but the whorls do not have a varix.
Exterior shell colour, yellowish-white, with purplish-brown lines on the ridges.

Giant Pacific Coast Bittium (*Bittium eschrichti*):
Alaska; Pacific coast Canada and U.S.A.
Occurs on lower shore.
Shell has up to 9 whorls, with several spiral grooves; deeply sutured; aperture oval.
Exterior shell colour, brownish-white.
Measures up to $\frac{1}{2}$-inch in length.

Needle Shell, Needle Whelk (*Bittium [Cerithium] reticulatum*):
South and west coast British Isles; Ireland.
Occurs on lower shore and below, on decaying seaweed and marine creatures, among debris, etc. May be present in large numbers.
Shell tall pointed spire; up to 16 whorls, with longitudinal ribs and up to 4 spiral crossing ridges, these forming pale coloured, coarse nodules that may be worn smooth on the shore; each whorl has a varix; apex twisted; near-round operculum; no umbilicus or notch at base.
Exterior shell colour, red-brown.
Measures up to $\frac{1}{2}$-inch in length, $\frac{1}{8}$-inch in width.

Californian Horn Shell (*Cerithidea californica*):
Pacific coast U.S.A. and Mexico.
Occurs on lower shore, on mudflats.
Shell tall spire; up to 10 whorls with weak spiral ridges and up to 18 axial or longitudinal ribs; deeply sutured; aperture lip swollen; aperture oval.
Exterior shell colour, dark brown, paler on whorl sutures and longitudinal ribs; aperture lip whitish.
Measures up to $1\frac{1}{4}$ inches in length.

False Cerith (*Batillaria minima*):
South-east coast U.S.A.; West Indies.
Occurs on lower shore, on mud.
Shell blunt pointed spire, more swollen, less narrow than similar shell species; up to 8 whorls, with longitudinal ribs and crossing ridges, these forming coarse nodules; sutures less deep; oval operculum.
Exterior shell colour, variable, greyish, blackish, with brownish-white, black or white alternate spiral bands.
Measures up to $\frac{1}{2}$-inch in length.

Florida Cerith (*Cerithium floridanum*):
South-east coast U.S.A.
Occurs on lower shore and below.
Shell pointed spire, up to 10 whorls, with longitudinal nodules and spiral broken ridges having a tubercled appearance; prominent siphonal canal; aperture oval; outer lip irregular.
Exterior shell colour, brown with white markings.
Measures up to an inch in length.

Reversed Horn Shell (*Triphora [Cerithium] perversa*):
South and west coast England; Channel Isles; Ireland: Scotland; Orkney and Shetland Isles.
Occurs on lower shore.
Shell tall pointed spire; sinistral, coiled with aperture to the left, not right as is usual; up to 16 whorls with small tubercles; shell base has 3 spiral ridges.
Exterior shell colour, yellowish-brown.
Measures up to $\frac{1}{3}$-inch in length.

Giant Pacific Coast Bittium
(*Bittium eschrichti*)

Needle Shell, Needle Whelk
(*Bittium [Cerithium] reticulatum*)

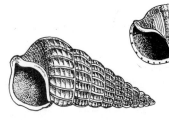

False Cerith (*Batillaria minima*)

Californian Horn Shell
(*Cerithidea californica*)

Reversed Horn Shell
(*Triphora [Cerithium] perversa*)

STAIRCASE SHELLS OR WENTLETRAPS

So-named because of a supposed resemblance to a spiral staircase,
'wentletrap' originating from a Dutch word meaning 'circular
staircase'. The tall spire of deep sutured whorls has a number of
obvious longitudinal ribs.

Brown-Banded Wentletrap (*Epitonium rupicola*)
East and south-east coast U.S.A.
Occurs on lower shore and below.
Shell tall spired; up to 8 rounded whorls with up to 18 longitudi-
nal ribs and several varices; deep sutured; aperture rounded; lip
swollen.
Exterior shell colour, brownish-white or yellow-brown with
wide brown bands, two on the body whorl, one on other whorls;
lip white.
Measures up to ½-inch in length.

Common Wentletrap (*Clathrus [Epitonium] clathrus*):
British Isles; Europe.
Occurs usually below lower shore, but occasionally comes on to

Common Wentletrap
(*Clathrus [Epitonium] clathrus*)

Brown-Banded Wentletrap
(*Epitonium rupicola*)

Turton's Wentletrap
(*Clathrus turtonis*)

lower shore.
Shell tall spire; up to 16 whorls; prominent longitudinal folded back ridges cross each whorl at right angles and not flattened against shell; 9 ridges on body whorl; whorls deeply separated by sutures; near-round aperture has a flat, projecting lip.
Exterior shell colour, cream or fawn, sometimes with several bands of brownish-purple streaks.
Measures up to $1\frac{1}{2}$ inches in length, $\frac{1}{2}$-inch wide.

Greenland Wentletrap (*Epitonium greenlandicum*):
North and east coast Canada; north-east coast U.S.A.
Occurs below lower shore.
Shell tall spire; up to 8 whorls, with up to 12 prominent longitudinal ribs crossing each whorl at right angles, whorls and flattened spiral ridges separated by deep sutures; near-round aperture has a projecting lip.
Exterior shell colour, chalky-white or greyish.
Measures up to an inch in length.

Money Wentletrap (*Epitonium indianorum*):
Alaska; Pacific coast Canada and U.S.A.
Occurs on lower shore and below.
Shell tall spire; up to 8 rounded whorls each with up to 14 slightly recurving ribs; deep sutures; near-round aperture.
Exterior shell colour, white.
Measures up to an inch in length.

Turton's Wentletrap (*Clathrus turtonis*):
British Isles.
Occurs below lower shore usually; empty shells washed ashore.
Shell tall spire; up to 16 whorls; prominent longitudinal ridges
crossing each whorl at right angles and flattened against shell;
greater number of ridges than in Common Wentletrap; 12 ridges
on body whorl; some of the ridges are double as wide varices.
Exterior shell colour, glossy, yellowish-brown, with several
purple-brown spiral bands on the whorls.
Measures up to $1\frac{3}{4}$ inches in length; $\frac{1}{2}$-inch wide.

Wroblewski's Wentletrap (*Opalia wroblewskii*):
Alaska; Pacific coast Canada; north-west coast U.S.A.
Occurs on lower shore and below.
Shell tall pointed spire; up to 8 whorls, with up to 8 prominent
longitudinal ribs crossing each whorl; body whorl has a single
spiral ridge at its base; aperture round.
Exterior shell colour, white.
Measures up to an inch in length.

Auger, Screw-Shell, Tower Shell (*Turritella communis*):
British Isles.
Occurs on lower shore and below, in muddy sand and gravel;
empty shells washed ashore.
Shell long, narrow, tapering, screw-like; up to 20 whorls, the
first 10 whorls from base including body whorl each having
three spiral ridges; pointed apex; small, round aperture.
Exterior shell colour, white or yellowish-brown.
Measures up to $2\frac{1}{4}$ inches in length, $\frac{3}{4}$-inch wide.

Grey Atlantic Auger (*Terebra cinerea*):
South-east coast U.S.A.; West Indies.
On lower shore and below, on sand.
Shell long, narrow, tapering; up to 12 straight-sided whorls and
fine, not deep, sutures; top half of each whorl has up to 50 slightly
prominent ribs, also very fine spiral ridges.
Exterior shell colour, brownish-grey or cream, with darker
brown markings underneath each suture.
Measures up to an inch in length.

Auger, Screw-Shell, Tower Shell
(*Turritella communis*)

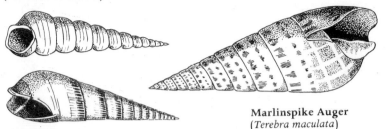

Marlinspike Auger
(*Terebra maculata*)

Grey Atlantic Auger
(*Terebra cinerea*)

Marlinspike Auger (*Terebra maculata*):
South-east Asia.
Occurs on lower shore.
Shell very long, narrow, tapering; up to 12 large whorls; pointed apex.
Exterior shell colour, brownish-white, with dark brown and mid-brown broken spiral bands.
Measures up to 10 inches in length.

American Pelican's Foot Shell (*Aporrhais occidentalis*):
East coast Canada and U.S.A.
Occurs below lower shore, in muddy sand.
Shell similar to Pelican's Foot Shell (*A. pes-pelecani*) except the expanded outer lip of the elongated aperture is not divided into ridged digits, but is one curving outer lip that has a similarity to some of the conches; the up to 8 rounded whorls each have up to 25 longitudinal ribs.
Exterior shell colour, brown, with paler aperture and exterior of long lip.
Measures up to 2 inches in length.

Pelican's Foot Shell (*Aporrhais pes-pelecani*)
British Isles; Atlantic coast Europe; Mediterranean.
Occurs on lower shore, in muddy sand and gravel; empty shells washed ashore.
Adult shell easily identified by the expanded outer lip of the elongated aperture, the divisions between the triangular digits,

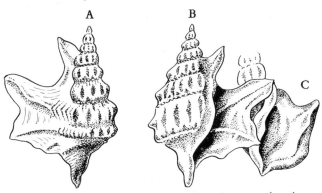

A, B **Pelican's Foot Shell** (*Aporrhais pes-pelecani*)
C **American Pelican's Foot Shell** (*Aporrhais occidentalis*)

which are ridged on their exterior, grooved on the interior, giving a supposed resemblance to a pelican's webbed foot. Several whorls ornamented with numerous tubercles. Immature examples shaped similar to the Ribbed Spindle Shell, with a curving outer lip and a straight canal at base.

Exterior shell colour, brownish or yellowish-white, sometimes tinged with lilac on the whorls; interior, yellowish-white. Measures up to $2\frac{1}{4}$ inches in length.

NECKLACE SHELLS (British Isles), NATICA SNAILS (U.S.A.) AND MOON SHELLS OR SNAILS (U.S.A.)

So-named because they form their egg masses in a gelatinous spiral circle, shaped like a collar, torque or necklace, into which sand grains become embedded to harden, camouflage and anchor it. The glossy, rounded shells are smooth, globular or oval, not unlike the garden snail (*Helix*) in shape, with a large umbilicus, spiral, ear-shaped operculum, large aperture and short, blunt spire. They are carnivorous and use their very large 'foot', which covers part of the shell, to dig under or climb upon and then grip the bivalve mollusc while using a proboscis to drill a round, bevelled-edge hole into the victim's shell and through this extract its soft contents. Usually found on sand, but empty shells are washed ashore.

146

Colourful Atlantic Natica
(*Natica canrena*)

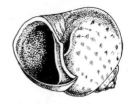

Common Necklace Shell
(*Natica alderi [poliana]*)

Large Necklace Shell
(*Natica catena [monilifera]*)

Lewis' Moon Snail
(*Lunatia lewisi*)

Colourful Atlantic Natica (*Natica canrena*):
East and south-east coast U.S.A.; West Indies.
Occurs on lower shore and below, in sand.
Shell rounded, glossy, smooth; the body whorl comprising nearly all the shell; slightly sutured; large oval aperture; grooved limy operculum.
Exterior shell colour, brownish-yellow with spiral rows of brown streaks and spots on paler bands on several whorls; internal callus and umbilicus, white.
Measures up to 2 inches in height.

Common Necklace Shell (*Natica alderi [poliana]*):
British Isles.
Occurs on lower shore and below.
Shell thick, rounded, glossy; up to 6 whorls; slightly sutured; short, blunt spire; aperture large, having a thick, broad, inner lip which forms a thick callus at aperture's top and a thick triangular pad in the middle which partly covers the narrow umbilicus.
Exterior shell colour, buff or yellowish-brown, with several spiral lines of reddish-brown or darker brownish spots, zig-zags

147

and streaks, body whorl having 5 rows.
Measures up to $\frac{3}{4}$-inch in height.

Common Northern Moon Snail (*Lunatia heros*):
North-east and east coast Canada; east coast U.S.A.
Occurs on lower shore and below.
Shell large, rounded-globular; body whorl comprising majority
of shell; slightly sutured; short blunt spire; large pear-shaped
aperture; small, deep umbilicus; thin periostracum.
Exterior shell colour, whitish-grey to pale brown; periostracum,
yellowish-brown.
Measures up to 4 inches in height.

Large Necklace Shell (*Natica catena* [*monilifera*]):
British Isles.
Occurs on lower shore and below.
Shell large, globular; up to 7 whorls; body whorl comprising
most of shell; wide inner lip has a solid white callus that projects
over the large, deep spiral-grooved umbilicus; short blunt spire.
Exterior shell colour, glossy yellowish-white, pale yellow or
buff, with a row of reddish-brown streaks or zig-zag marks on
each whorl, the last whorl sometimes having two rows of streaks
on its periphery.
Measures up to $1\frac{1}{2}$ inches in height.

Lewis' Moon Snail (*Lunatia lewisi*):
Pacific coast Canada and U.S.A.
Occurs on lower shore and below, in sand.
Shell large, rounded-globular; body whorl has a raised shoulder
and forms the greater part of the shell; narrow, deep umbilicus
with a button-like callus; large pear-shaped aperture; horny
operculum.
Exterior shell colour, whitish-brown; operculum, brown; callus,
brown; interior of aperture, whitish.
Measures up to 4 inches in height.

VIOLET SEA SNAILS (British Isles), JANTHINA SNAILS (U.S.A.)

These univalve molluscs are pelagic, living at the surface of the sea. They create a raft from gelatinous mucus in which air bubbles are trapped to keep it buoyant and to which the mollusc is attached upside-down by its 'foot', floating at the mercy of the currents and direction of the wind. If cast upon the shore, sometimes in hundreds after stormy weather, because of the mucus raft and weak, frail body these Sea Snails cannot make their way on their 'foot' back to the sea and soon die. Their colour varies from purple or dark violet to a pale lavender, with white. There are several species, but one most frequently occurring is the beautiful **Violet Sea Snail**, also known as **Purple Sea Snail (British Isles), Common Janthina (U.S.A.)** (*Janthina janthina*), with a light, thin, fragile, rather flattened shell, the body whorl forming most of the shell. Occurs by accident on the lower shore of the Atlantic coast of the British Isles, more so south-west England, also Ireland and the Pacific and Atlantic coasts of the U.S.A. Exterior shell colour, white-tinted mauve shading to a deep violet or purplish-blue. Measures up to $\frac{3}{4}$-inch in height, British Isles; $1\frac{1}{2}$ inches in height, U.S.A. Another example is the **Pallid Janthina** (*Janthina pallida*) which is more globular, less flattened, with a rounded aperture. It is pale whitish-violet in exterior colour and measures up to an inch in height.

Violet Sea Snails (British Isles), Janthina Snails (U.S.A.)

6 More Univalves

The thick, empty shells of some species of Whelk are as familiar on the shore zones as Periwinkles and Top Shells. They vary considerably among the species, being proportionately narrow compared to their height, with a pointed spire and large, siphonate, oval aperture and operculum, other species having a compressed spire with a very long tapering aperture, such as the Fulgur Whelks. Whelks are carnivorous and also scavengers. The colour of the shell may partly depend on the diet. If feeding entirely on mussels it may be dark brown or mauvish, while in those feeding on barnacles the shell may be dull white. (See Dog Whelk or Dog Winkle, *N. lapillus*.) Several species, particularly the Common Whelk, are used as human food, as they have been in Europe for centuries. Fishermen use them as cod bait, while the empty shells are adapted by hermit crabs for use as protective 'homes'.

Buckie, Red Whelk (*Neptunea antiqua*):
British Isles.
Occurs below lower shore, but empty shells occasionally washed ashore.
Shell thick, spindle-shaped, smoother surfaced than Common Whelk, but has numerous slight spiralled ridges on the up to 8 prominent whorls; large aperture has long siphonal canal; periostracum often worn off; abnormalities occur, particularly sinistral.
Exterior shell colour, yellowish, whitish, reddish or flesh. A variation 'alba', with expanded body whorl, is pure white, while another variation, 'ventricosa', has a dark orange interior.
Measures up to 6 inches in length.

Common Edible Whelk, Buckie, Kidney-Buckie (British Is.)
Common Northern Whelk or Buccinum (U.S.A.)

(*Buccinum undatum*):

British Isles; Ireland; Europe; north and east coast Canada; north-east coast U.S.A.

Occurs on lower shore and below, on gravel, muddy sand; empty shells common on this and other shore zones.

Shell variable, less spindle-shaped than Red Whelk (*N. antiqua*) up to 8 deeply sutured, sculptured whorls, with curved, broad ribs; body whorl more rounded; pointed apex; large, oval aperture has wide, short siphonal canal. There are several variations, the most frequent being 'littoralis', having a large, swollen body whorl, short spire and brownish-purple or orange interior; abnormalities occur, particularly sinistral, or with unusually long spire or body whorl.

Exterior shell colour, white-yellowish or pale brownish; white examples on shore may have periostracum worn away or if lying a considerable time be bleached by the sun.

Measures up to 6 inches in length offshore, usually about 3 inches or less on shore.

Glacial Whelk (*Buccinum glaciale*):

Alaska; north, west and east coast Canada.

Occurs below lower shore.

Shell shape similar to Common Buccinum or Whelk (*B. undatum*); up to 6 deeply sutured whorls, finely sculptured; body whorl less rounded, narrower, irregular in outline; has two prominent spiral ridges; aperture smaller, narrower, with a short siphonal canal; thick, flared outer lip.

Exterior shell colour, mauvish-brown.

Measures up to 2 inches in length.

New England Neptune (*Neptunea decemcostata*):

East coast Canada; north-east coast U.S.A.

Occurs on lower shore and below, on rocks.

Shell typical whelk shape, but has up to 10 very prominent spiral ridges on whorls; upper whorls may have 2 ridges; large aperture oval with long siphonal canal.

Exterior shell colour, greyish-white to yellowish-brown with red-brown spiral ridges; aperture, greyish-white.

Measures up to 4 inches in length.

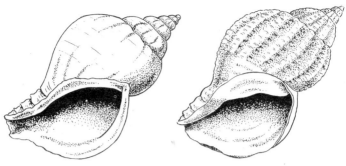

Buckie, Red Whelk
(*Neptunea antiqua*)

Common Edible Whelk, Buckie, Kidney-Buckie (British Isles), Common Northern Whelk or Buccinum (U.S.A.)
(*Buccinum undatum*)

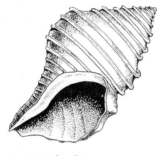

New England Neptune
(*Neptunea decemcostata*)

Glacial Whelk (*Buccinum glaciale*)

North West Neptune (*Neptunea lyrata*):
Alaska; north and west coast Canada; north-west coast U.S.A. Occurs on lower shore and below.
Shell shape similar to New England Neptune, but has up to 9 irregular spiral ridges and weaker spiral ridges; large aperture oval, with wavy outer lip.
Exterior shell colour, dull brown; lip and aperture, darker brown. Measures up to 5 inches in length.

FULGUR WHELKS

These Whelks prey on the Hard Shell Clams which they force open by use of their large 'foot' and shell, feeding on them through a long proboscis.

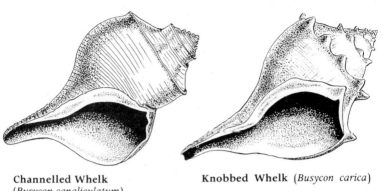

Channelled Whelk
(*Busycon canaliculatum*)

Knobbed Whelk (*Busycon carica*)

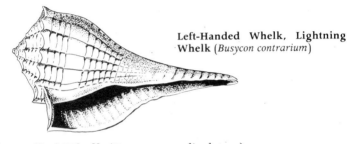

Left-Handed Whelk, Lightning Whelk (*Busycon contrarium*)

Channelled Whelk (*Busycon canaliculatum*):
East coast U.S.A.
Occurs on lower shore and below, on sand.
Shell elongated; up to 5 almost flat-topped, finely-ridged whorls; shoulders of whorls have a keel; deeply-channelled suture; body whorl large and tapering, with large, oval aperture and elongated siphonal canal; compressed spire.
Exterior shell colour, dull whitish-brown; aperture, brownish.
Measures up to 7 inches in length.

Knobbed Whelk (*Busycon carica*):
East coast U.S.A.
Occurs on lower shore and below.
Shell elongated; up to 5 whorls; body whorl large and tapering, with long aperture and siphonal canal; two largest whorls have several nodules or 'knobs' on the shoulders.
Exterior shell colour, dirty greenish-white; aperture creamy-white to orange-red.
Measures up to 8 inches in length.

Left-Handed Whelk, Lightning Whelk (*Busycon contrarium*):
East and south-east coast U.S.A.
Occurs on lower shore and below.
Shell elongated; up to 5 ridged whorls; body whorl large and has a very long taper with large aperture and long narrow siphonal canal; body whorl has nodules or 'knobs' on the shoulder but these are not so big as Knobbed Whelk (*B. carica*); compressed spire; as name describes, shell is sinistral or left-handed.
Exterior shell colour, white; young examples have longitudinal brown streaks.
Measures up to 16 inches in length.

Pear Whelk (*Busycon spiratum*):
South-east coast U.S.A.
Occurs on lower shore and below.
Shell elongated; up to 5 finely ridged whorls; similar in shape to Channelled Whelk; body whorl large and tapering, but no nodules or 'knobs'; long, oval aperture and siphonal canal; V-shaped suture channel. A variation 'plagosum' has keeled shoulders, another, 'pyruloides' has rounded, smooth whorls.
Exterior shell colour, creamy-brown or tan, with longitudinal darker brown markings.
Measures up to 5 inches in length.

DOG WHELKS (British Isles),
NASSA MUD SNAILS (U.S.A.)

The Dog Whelks or Nassas have smaller shells than the familiar Whelks and some species are gregarious and very common. The shell has a short siphonal canal and pronounced spire. If living specimens are found they can be identified from the Drills or Sting Winkles by the expanded 'foot' being divided into two fleshy prolongations or 'tails' at its posterior end instead of being blunt. They are active scavengers, feeding on dead, decaying animal matter, keeping the shore zones free of such material, and are sometimes lured to fishermens' bait or that in lobster and crab pots by the odour of dead flesh in the water, detected by the snail's smell sensory organ, the osphradium, after inhaling the water through the siphon.

Eastern Mud Nassa
(*Ilyanassa obsoleta*)

Giant Western Nassa
(*Nassarius fossatus*)

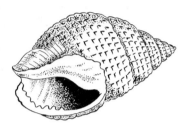
Netted Dog Whelk
(*Nassarius reticulatus*)

Thick-Lipped Dog Whelk
(*Nassarius incrassatus*)

Common Eastern Nassa (*Nassarius vibex*):
East coast U.S.A.; West Indies.
Occurs on lower shore, on muddy sand.
Shell rounded, up to 6 whorls, with beaded, longitudinal ribs and
fine spiral ridges; aperture oval, with parietal shield thick glazed.
Exterior shell colour, greyish, with narrow brown bands;
parietal shield, yellowish-white.
Measures up to $\frac{1}{2}$-inch in length.

Eastern Mud Nassa (*Ilyanassa obsoleta*):
East coast Canada, U.S.A.; west coast Canada, U.S.A.
Occurs on lower shore, on mudflats.
Shell with network appearance of intersecting ribs and spiral
ridges, but weak, flattened beads not prominent; up to 5 rounded
whorls; spire eroded; aperture oval; parietal wall glazed; ridge
near base of columella; posterior 'foot' does not have the two
fleshy prolongations or cirri.
Exterior shell colour, yellowish-brown; parietal wall, purple-
brown.
Measures up to $\frac{3}{4}$-inch in length.

Giant Western Nassa (*Nassarius fossatus*):
Pacific coast Canada, U.S.A., Mexico.
Occurs on lower shore.
Shell rounded, up to 6 whorls, with beaded, longitudinal ribs and spiral ridges; deep sutured; aperture oval; wide siphonal canal; pointed apex.
Exterior shell colour, pale brown, brownish-white, orange-brown.
Measures up to 2 inches in length.

Netted Dog Whelk (*Nassarius reticulatus*):
British Isles.
Occurs on lower shore and below, on sand and muddy sand; in shallow pools on sand after tide has receded.
Shell thick, with prominent network appearance of strong inter-secting ribs and spiral striae; up to 10 whorls; 6 spiral ridges on broad grooved base; aperture has up to 12 tooth-like projections on inside of crenated outer lip; pointed spire.
Exterior shell colour, buff, orange-yellowish or pale brown, with a purplish-brown banding on the whorls; aperture, white.
Measures up to $1\frac{1}{2}$ inches in length.

Thick-Lipped Dog Whelk (*Nassarius incrassatus*):
British Isles; Channel Isles.
Occurs on lower shore and below, on rocks, stones and gravel.
Shell thick, more rounded than Netted Dog Whelk; up to 9 whorls; has prominent, up to 18, longitudinal ribs crossed at right-angles with spiral striae; outer lip thick and swollen.
Exterior shell colour, variable, usually brownish, with darker reddish-brown bands and a brown marking on base; also whitish-yellow, various pinks, purple, buff or orange, striped or mottled with brown markings; pointed apex usually pink or purplish; dark spot on the canal; aperture, white.
Measures up to $\frac{3}{4}$-inch in length.

Western Mud Nassa (*Nassarius tegula*):
Pacific coast U.S.A.; Mexico.
Occurs on lower shore, on mudflats.
Shell rounded; up to 6 whorls, finely ridged; nodules or 'knobs' beneath the suture; parietal wall glazed; pointed spire.

Exterior shell colour, brownish, but may have up to 3 paler, yellowish band markings on larger whorls; parietal wall, white. Measures up to $\frac{1}{2}$-inch in length.

DOG WINKLES, DRILLS AND PURPURAS

These have the familiar Whelk or Periwinkle shell shape. The thick shell sometimes has a rugged, sculptured appearance, with a siphonated aperture, oval operculum and pointed spire. These molluscs are carnivorous, using a long proboscis with a rasping radula, to extend through the opening of a 'false mouth' to bore a round, straight-sided hole into the shell of a victim and extract the contents, or, using their 'foot' and shell, they force open bivalves for the same purpose. Related to the Murex group some species contain the fluid used in ancient times as a purple dye, and by the mollusc to defend itself. They are found in shallow water in the habitats of their prey.

American Oyster Drill, American Whelk Tingle (British Isles), Atlantic Oyster Drill (U.S.A.) (*Urosalpinx cinerea*):
Kent, Essex, south-east coast England; north-west coast Europe; east coast Canada; east and south-east coast U.S.A.; Pacific coast U.S.A.
Occurs below lower shore, in oyster beds, where it is a serious pest; imported with American Oysters (*C. virginica*) used to restock dwindling Native English beds; also preys on other bivalves.
Shell similar to Sting Winkle (*O. erinacea*), smoother; no varices; up to 7 whorls, with up to 12 rounded, less prominent, longitudinal ribs with numerous crossing, spiral striae; siphonal canal open; pointed apex.
Exterior shell colour, whitish, pale greyish-brown, sometimes with brownish spiral bands.
Measures up to $1\frac{1}{4}$ inches in length, $\frac{3}{4}$-inches wide.

Common Dog Whelk, Dog Winkle, Purple (British Isles), Atlantic Dog Winkle (U.S.A.), Horse Winkle (Ireland) (*Nucella [Purpura] lapillus*):
British Isles; Ireland; north-east and east coast Canada; east coast U.S.A.

American Oyster Drill, American Whelk Tingle (British Isles), Atlantic Oyster Drill (U.S.A.) (*Urosalpinx cinerea*)

Common Dog Whelk, Dog Winkle, Purple (British Isles), Atlantic Dog Winkle (U.S.A.), Horse Winkle (Ireland) (*Nucella [Purpura] lapillus*)

Occurs on the middle and lower shore zones, with barnacles, limpets, periwinkles, top shells and mussels and in oyster beds, also on dead animal matter; may be exposed on rocks when tide recedes.

Shell thick, cone shaped; has numerous flat, spiral ridges; short spire; deep canal; large aperture, outer lip with tubercles on inside margin. Shell variable with habitat and in sheltered places may have longer spire and small aperture.

Exterior shell colour, variable, dull white, yellow, orange, brown, lilac; if feeding on mussels may be darker and spirally banded with orange or dark brown; if feeding mainly on barnacles colour dull white. Examples may also be white and black, like humbug sweets, or yellowish-brown banded with dark brown; a mixed diet or change of diet has been suggested as a cause.

Measures up to $1\frac{1}{2}$ inches in length, an inch wide, British Isles, up to 2 inches in length, U.S.A.

Emarginate Dog Winkle (*Nucella emarginata*):
Alaska; Pacific coast, Canada, U.S.A., Mexico.
Occurs on lower shore, on rocks.

Shell with numerous, pronounced, spiral ridges which are alternately thick and thin to short spire; large oval aperture; arched, flattened columella.

Exterior shell colour, brown with whitish spiral bands; columella and aperture, pale brown.

Measures up to an inch in length.

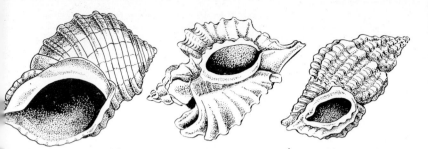

Emarginate Dog Winkle
(*Nucella emarginata*)

Foliated Thorn Purpura
(*Ceratostoma foliata*)

Sting Winkle or Drill
(*Ocenebra* [*Murex*] *erinacea*)

Foliated Thorn Purpura (*Ceratostoma foliata*):
Alaska; Pacific coast Canada and U.S.A.
Occurs on lower shore, on rocks.
Shell unmistakable due to the three, thin, wing-like, spreading, wavy, ribbed varices giving it an irregular, deformed shape; up to 5 whorls; pointed spire; almost encircled aperture oval; outer lip has a spine.
Exterior shell colour, brownish.
Measures up to 2 inches in length.

Sting Winkle or Drill (*Ocenebra* [*Murex*] *erinacea*):
South and west coast England; Wales; Ireland.
Occurs on lower shore and below, with barnacles, mussels, and other bivalves, a pest in oyster beds.
Shell, thick, rugged, more pointed than Dog Winkle (*N. lapillus*) with prominent, rugose, longitudinal, varicose ribs crossed by several spiral ridges from aperture to pointed apex; up to 10 whorls; deep sutures; siphonal canal closed in mature examples, open in young; aperture with several small tubercles on inside. Despite name has no 'sting', only the proboscis.
Exterior shell colour, dull white, yellowish-white, with dark streaks.
Measures up to 2 inches in length, an inch wide.

A relative, **Small Sting Winkle or Crinkly Dog Whelk** (*Ocenebra aciculata*) occurs on lower shore and below only in the Channel Isles.
Smaller, spindle-shaped shell has longitudinal ribs and numerous fine, spiral ridges, up to 8 whorls. Colour dark reddish-brown and up to $\frac{1}{2}$-inch in length, $\frac{1}{4}$-inch wide.

LITTLE SPINDLE SHELLS (British Isles), TROPHON SHELLS (U.S.A.) AND MANGELIA SHELLS

The Spindle Shells or Trophons are similar to their Whelk, Dog Winkle and Drill relatives in shape, but most are much smaller. They are also carnivorous, using a proboscis with radula to penetrate the victim's shell for the contents.

The Mangelia Shells are similar to the Spindle Shells but are much more slender and elongated, with a narrow aperture. Another difference is they do not usually have an operculum; also the outer lip has no grooves on its interior.

Orpheus Trophon (*Boreotrophon orpheus*):
Alaska; Pacific coast Canada and U.S.A.
Occurs below lower shore, on stony seabed.
Shell slender, up to 5 whorls, with prominent, longitudinal ribs crossed by finer spiral ridges; deep suture; aperture large oval, with long, open siphonal canal.
Exterior shell colour, white.
Measures up to $\frac{1}{2}$-inch in length.

Prickly Spindle Shell (*Trophon muricatus*):
South-west coast England; south coast Ireland; Isle of Man; Channel Isles.
Occurs below lower shore.
Shell slender, up to 8 turreted whorls, crossed by numerous swollen, longitudinal ribs not joined to sutures, with fine, spiral striae forming channels; where ribs and striae meet there are tubercles or prickles; aperture oval, small with long open canal; operculum pear-shaped.
Exterior shell colour, flesh-pink or yellowish-white.
Measures up to $\frac{1}{2}$-inch in length, $\frac{3}{16}$-inch wide.

Ribbed Spindle Shell (*Trophon truncatus*):
British Isles, but scarce on south coast of England; Isle of Man; south-east coast Ireland; Atlantic coast Europe; Mediterranean.
Occurs below lower shore.
Shell slightly broader than *T. muricatus*; up to 7 whorls, the

Plate IX The **Ramose Murex** (*Murex ramosus*)

Plate X Two Conchs. On the left the
Silver Conch (*Strombus lentigino-
sus*); on the right the **Florida
Fighting Conch** (*Strombus alatus*)

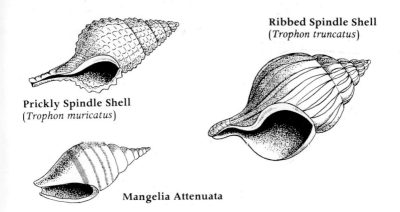

Prickly Spindle Shell
(*Trophon muricatus*)

Ribbed Spindle Shell
(*Trophon truncatus*)

Mangelia Attenuata

numerous longitudinal ribs do not have tubercles or prickles; upper part of shell smooth, glossy; aperture larger, more rounded with a shorter, open canal.
Exterior shell colour, flesh or yellowish-white.
Measures up to $\frac{3}{4}$-inch in length, $\frac{5}{16}$-inch wide.

Mangelia Attenuata:
South coast England; Atlantic coast Europe; Mediterranean.
Occurs below lower shore; empty shells are occasionally washed ashore.
Shell slender; up to 9 whorls; deep sutures; up to 10 prominent ribs; aperture long oval.
Exterior shell colour, pale brown-orange with reddish-brown lines, chestnut-red band below the periphery; ribs usually paler brown than other parts of the shell.
Measures up to $\frac{1}{2}$-inch in length.

Mangelia Nebula:
British Isles.
Occurs on lower shore and below.
Shell slender cone-shape; up to 11 whorls, up to 12 prominent longitudinal ribs and fine spiral striae.
Exterior shell colour, chocolate-brown; ribs usually paler brown than other parts of the shell.
Measures up to $\frac{1}{2}$-inch in length.

MUREX SHELLS

This family contains some of the most spectacular shell shapes, keenly sought by collectors. The shell is usually heavy, thick and sometimes long spined or frilled. Most are tropical molluscs, carnivorous, chiefly on bivalves, in shallow water. A gland on the mantle produces a fluid which changes to a permanent deep purple on being exposed to sunlight. This is the well-known Royal Tyrian Purple dye used by the Romans, Greeks and others to create ceremonial garments in this colour. The mollusc has a more mundane use for the fluid. Its foul smell is thought to act upon their victims like an anaesthetic.

Apple Murex (*Murex pomum*):
South-east coast U.S.A.; Caribbean; Brazil.
Occurs on lower shore, in shallow water.
Shell thick; irregularly ribbed and knobbed in outline, but no long spines; aperture oval.
Exterior shell colour, brownish-yellow or brown-white, with darker markings; outer lip has brown spots; inner lip parietal wall yellowish, red-brown or orange, the upper end having a dark brownish spot.
Measures up to $2\frac{1}{2}$ inches in length.

Gem Murex (*Maxwellia gemma*):
Pacific coast U.S.A., Mexico.
Occurs on lower shore, in shallow water, among rocks.
Shell thick, with 6 rounded, smooth varices on body whorl; spire has squarish, deep pits; aperture rounded.
Exterior shell colour, bluish or blackish markings on white.
Measures up to an inch in length.

Giant Atlantic or Eastern Murex (*Murex fulvescens*):
East and south-east coast U.S.A.; Gulf of Mexico.
Occurs on lower shore and below; in shallow water during spawning.
Shell thick, heavy, with numerous short, tough spines on the varices.
Exterior shell colour, dull white.
Measures up to 5 inches in length.

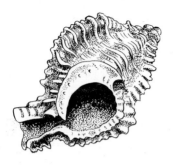

Apple Murex (*Murex pomum*)   **Gem Murex** (*Maxwellia gemma*)

Lace Murex (*Murex dilectus*):
South-east coast U.S.A.; West Indies.
Occurs on lower shore and below, in shallow water.
Shell thick; irregular, with very spiny varices; aperture nearly round, small.
Exterior shell colour, variable, brownish, dull whitish; apex has pink tint.
Measures up to $2\frac{1}{2}$ inches in length.

Pink-Mouthed Murex (*Murex erythrostomus*):
Pacific coast U.S.A.; Central America.
Occurs on lower shore and below, on sandy mud.
Shell thick, with a few short, tough spines; large, oval aperture; short siphonal canal; unmistakable due to coloration.
Exterior shell colour, white; outer and inner lip, a delicate pink.
Measures up to 6 inches in length.

Purple Dye Murex (*Murex brandaris*):
Mediterranean.
Occurs below lower shore.
Shell thick, with a few short, tough spines; aperture oval in centre of prominent lips; long siphonal canal.
Exterior shell colour, white.
Measures up to 3 inches in length.

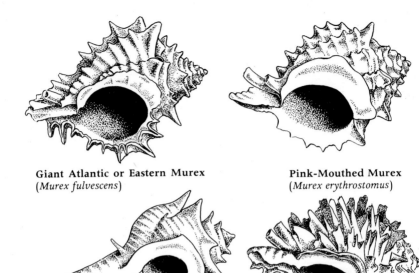

Giant Atlantic or Eastern Murex
(*Murex fulvescens*)

Pink-Mouthed Murex
(*Murex erythrostomus*)

Purple Dye Murex
(*Murex brandaris*)

Radix Murex (*Murex radix*)

Radix Murex (*Murex radix*):
Pacific coast U.S.A.; Central America.
Occurs on lower shore and below, on sandy mud.
Shell thick, with numerous spines on whorls, including outer lip; large, oval aperture; short siphonal canal.
Exterior shell colour, brownish-white, with dark brownish – black spines.
Measures up to 4 inches in length.

Ramose Murex (*Murex ramosus*):
Indo-Pacific.
Occurs on lower shore and below, in shallow water.
Shell thick, heavy, with numerous blunt spines on the large body whorl and smaller whorls, including outer lip; large oval aperture, with irregular outer lip; lengthy siphonal canal.
Exterior shell colour, white, with brown on body whorl, smaller whorls and outer lip, though some specimens may have little brown or be all-white; aperture margin pink; aperture white.
Measures up to 12 inches in length.

TRITON SHELLS

Some examples of this family are so large they are used as a trumpet by native fishermen to contact each other, while in South America and Japan they are used as a musical instrument at religious services. Pacific examples have been used as cooking vessels. A few occur in cold water regions but the majority are tropical. They are carnivorous and feed mainly on Starfish. The Hairy Tritons are so-called because they have a horny or 'hairy' periostracum to protect their shell from penetration by Boring Sponges.

Angular Triton (*Cymatium femorale*):
South-east coast U.S.A.; Caribbean; Brazil.
Occurs on lower shore and below.
Shell thick; knobbed; with large, wing-shaped varices and numerous spiral ridges; aperture long oval; inner lip smooth.
Exterior shell colour, pale brown; reddish; orange; with darker bands; outer lip has prominent white 'knobs'; inner lip, white.
Measures up to 6 inches in length.

Atlantic Triton, Triton's Trumpet (*Charonia variegata*):
South-east coast U.S.A.; Caribbean; West Indies.
Occurs on lower shore and below, in coral reefs.
Shell thick; not unlike a very large Common Whelk in shape; large body whorl; pointed, tapering apex; aperture large, oval; outer lip has pairs of small 'teeth'; inner lip numerous uneven ridges.
Exterior shell colour, white, but amount variable; with brown spiral patterning; outer lip 'teeth', white; inner lip, dark or mid-brown, ridges white; interior, white or orange-brown.
Measures up to 12 inches in length, but Pacific variety may be up to 18 inches in length.

Common Hairy Triton (*Cymatium pileare*):
South-east coast U.S.A.; Caribbean; Brazil: South-east Asia.
Occurs below lower shore, on coral reefs.
Shell thick, with rounded varices; ridges beaded small aperture oval with narrow, raised 'teeth' on the inner lip and outer lip; periostracum thick and matted.

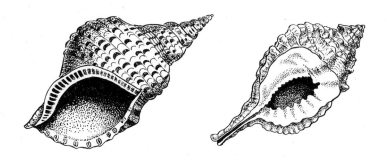

Atlantic Triton, Triton's Trumpet
(*Charonia variegata*)

Knobbed Triton
(*Cymatium muricinum*)

Exterior shell colour, brown, with lighter and darker spiral bandings; aperture reddish-brown; 'teeth' white; aperture interior similar to exterior.
Measures up to 4 inches in length.

Knobbed Triton (*Cymatium muricinum*):
South-east coast U.S.A.; Caribbean; Brazil.
Occurs on lower shore and below, on coral reefs.
Shell thick, with irregular ridges; small aperture oval with raised 'teeth' on the inner lip and outer lip; long siphonal canal.
Exterior shell colour, whitish-grey or brownish; aperture interior, brown.
Measures up to $1\frac{1}{2}$ inches in length.

Knobbed Triton's Trumpet (*Charonia nodifera*):
Mediterranean.
Occurs below lower shore.
Shell thick; not unlike very large Common Whelk in shape; large body whorl; pointed, tapering apex; long oval aperture; outer lip has several 'teeth', inner lip smooth.
Exterior shell colour, brownish-white, with darker spiral markings; outer lip, white, with prominent brown marks; inner lip, white; aperture interior, white.
Measures up to 16 inches in length.

CONCH SHELLS

The Conch Shells are probably most people's idea of a tropical shell – quite large and beautifully coloured. The majority are in fact tropical, occurring in warm, shallow water, on sandy mud bottoms. Characteristic of the Conches is the expanded outer lip, on the lower part of which is a rounded, 'stromboid' notch. They feed on algae and are themselves gathered for human consumption.

Florida Fighting Conch (*Strombus alatus*):
South-east coast U.S.A.; Mexico.
Occurs on lower shore and below, on sandy mud.
Shell thick; very large, glossy, body whorl has several blunt knobs; knobs also on the other whorls; short spines on spire; outer lip slopes downwards from top of body whorls.
Exterior shell colour, white, mottled or banded yellow, reddish-purple and orange-brown; outer lip, similar. Occasionally albino specimens are found.
Measures up to 3 inches in length.

Hawk-Wing Conch (*Strombus raninus*):
South-east coast U.S.A.; Caribbean; West Indies.
Occurs on lower shore.
Shell thick; very large, glossy, body whorl, but only a few blunt knobs on it; outer lip points upwards rising above junction with top of body whorl, like an outstretched wing; some examples have this extension more pointed, others are rounded or irregular.
Exterior shell colour, white, variably mottled with purples and browns; outer lip, whitish; aperture interior, reddish-brown.
Measures up to 4 inches in length.

Queen Conch, Pink Conch (*Strombus gigas*):
South-east coast U.S.A.; Caribbean; West Indies; Brazil.
Occurs on lower shore and below, on sand.
Shell thick, heavy; very large, glossy, body whorl; with blunt knobs on all whorls; thick outer lip extends the full length of the shell, with top rounded and also may be equally as wide as re-

167

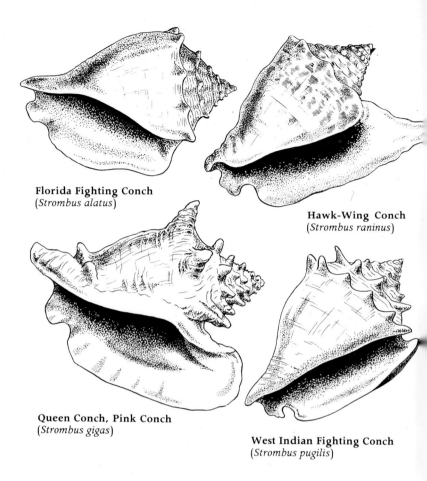

Florida Fighting Conch
(*Strombus alatus*)

Hawk-Wing Conch
(*Strombus raninus*)

Queen Conch, Pink Conch
(*Strombus gigas*)

West Indian Fighting Conch
(*Strombus pugilis*)

mainder of shell. Extremely beautiful and unmistakable. Occasionally pink or reddish semi-precious pearls have been found inside those harvested for food.

Exterior shell colour, pale brownish-white or yellowish, the aperture, inner lip and outer lip, except yellow-white margin, is a delicate rose-pink.

Measures up to 12 inches in length.

Silver Conch (*Strombus lentiginosus*):
Indo-Pacific.
Occurs on lower shore and below.
Shell thick; large body whorl, with several spiral rows of a few,

low, blunt knobs on it, the largest knobs being at the shoulder; a few smaller knobs on other whorls; thick outer lip extends the full length of the shell, but more curved, with several indentations.

Exterior shell colour, white, with pale to dark brown and greyish blotches and larger areas; outer lip indentations brown; aperture white and pinkish-brown.

Measures up to 3 inches in length.

West Indian Fighting Conch (*Strombus pugilis*):
South-east coast U.S.A.; Caribbean; Brazil.
Occurs on lower shore.
Shell thick; large, glossy body whorl with blunt knobs, the next to last whorl having some long spines unless worn down or broken; outer lip not so extensive, but has an obvious slope upwards at the top.

Exterior shell colour, pale yellowish-brown; body whorl and outer lip, orange-brown; aperture interior, whitish.

Measures up to 3 inches in length.

HELMET AND BONNET SHELLS

Larger examples of the Helmet Shells are those most frequently used for the creation of shell cameos. They occur chiefly in tropical areas, on sandy bottoms in shallow water. They are identified by the area alongside the inner margin of the aperture, the parietal shield, being extended. The whorls also usually have a varix at spaced intervals. Sea Urchins are their main prey.

The Bonnet Shells are rounded, the parietal shield more oval than triangular, with no varix on the whorls.

Emperor Helmet, Queen Helmet (*Cassis madagascariensis*):
South-east coast U.S.A.; West Indies.
Occurs on lower shore and below, on sand.
Shell thick, heavy, glossy; several blunt 'knobs' on shoulder of body whorl; parietal shield large and triangular, with inner side rounded; numerous 'teeth' on aperture margin.

Exterior shell colour, pale brown; parietal shield, yellowish; dark brown or black between 'teeth'.

Measures up to 14 inches in length.

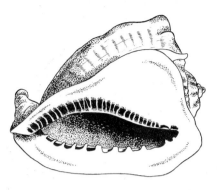

Flame Helmet (*Cassis flammea*)

Emperor Helmet, Queen Helmet
(*Cassis madagascariensis*)

Flame Helmet (*Cassis flammea*):
South-east coast U.S.A.; Gulf of Mexico; Brazil.
Occurs on lower shore.
Shell thick, glossy; numerous 'knobs' on whorls; parietal shield triangular-oval and flat; numerous prominent 'teeth' on aperture margin.
Exterior shell colour, mottled browns, yellows, mauves; parietal shield, whitish or yellowish with a mottled area; 'teeth' have no dark brown or black between them.
Measures up to 4 inches in length.

King Helmet (*Cassis tuberosa*):
East and south-east coast U.S.A.; Caribbean; Brazil.
Occurs on lower shore and below, on or partly in sand.
Shell thick, heavy, glossy; several blunt 'knobs' on body whorl; parietal shield large, flat and triangular; numerous 'teeth' on aperture margin.
Exterior shell colour, brownish; parietal shield, whitish or yellowish; black between 'teeth'; several dark brown stripes or blotches on outer lip near 'teeth', also brownish area on inner lip's aperture margin.
Measures up to 7 inches in length.

Prickly Helmet (*Galeodea echinophora*):
Mediterranean.
Occurs on and below lower shore.

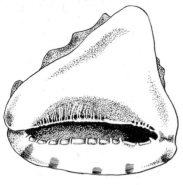

King Helmet (*Cassis tuberosa*)

Prickly Helmet
(*Galeodea echinophora*)

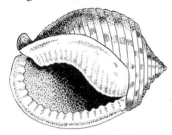

Scotch Bonnet (*Phalium granulatum*)

Tuscan Helmet (*Galeodea rugosa*)

Shell rounded, with a large body whorl; spirally ridged with several thicker and raised; aperture large, long-oval; parietal wall of inner lip broad, smooth; outer lip narrower.
Exterior shell colour, white, with pale lilac lines or broken lines on raised ridges; inner and outer lip, white.
Measures up to 3 inches in length.

Scotch Bonnet (*Phalium granulatum*):
East and south-east coast U.S.A.; Caribbean; Mexico; Brazil.
Occurs on lower shore, on sand.
Shell rounded; very large body whorl; whorls with numerous spiral grooves which are beaded and variable in width; parietal wall broad with numerous small pustules; aperture's outer lip margin toothed; aperture long-oval.
Exterior shell colour, pale pinkish with broken brown or reddish-brown spiral markings; outer lip, white; inner lip, white with a few pale brown markings.
Measures up to 3 inches in length.

171

Smooth Scotch Bonnet (*Phalium cicatricosum*):
South-east coast U.S.A.; Caribbean; Brazil.
Occurs on lower shore, on sand.
Shell rounded, similar to Scotch Bonnet, but smooth and without grooves; parietal wall also has small pustules; aperture's outer lip margin toothed; aperture long-oval.
Exterior shell colour, pale brownish, the brown spiral markings being almost continuous; outer lip, white; inner lip, white, with a few pale brown markings.
Measures up to 3 inches in length.

Tuscan Helmet (*Galeodea rugosa*):
Mediterranean.
Occurs on and below lower shore.
Shell rounded, with a large body whorl; spirally ridged; aperture large, long-oval; parietal wall of inner lip broad, smooth; outer lip narrower.
Exterior shell colour, white.
Measures up to 3 inches in length.

TULIP SHELLS, TULIP CONCHS OR BAND SHELLS AND HORSE CONCH

This group, which also includes the Large Spindle Shells or Fusinus, contains the largest gastropod shell in United States waters, the Florida Horse Conch, which, when adult, reaches 20 inches in length. It is becoming rare to find it this size, however, due to too much collecting of the species before it matures. The Tulip and Horse Conchs are not unlike elongated Common Whelks; they are carnivorous, feeding on bivalves.

Banded Tulip (*Fasciolaria hunteria*):
East and south-east coast U.S.A.
Occurs on lower shore, in shallow water, on sandy mud.
Shell thick; large body whorl; smooth whorls; deep suture; long siphonal canal; aperture narrow, long-oval.
Exterior shell colour, pale mauvish-brown or bluish-green, with narrow, irregular pale orange-yellow or brownish spiral markings overlaid by a continual thin, brown spiral line from apex

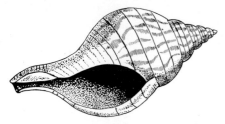

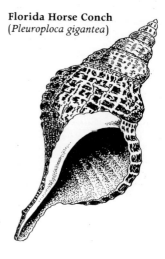

Florida Horse Conch
(*Pleuroploca gigantea*)

Banded Tulip (*Fasciolaria hunteria*)

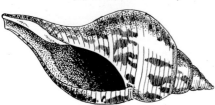

True Tulip (*Fasciolaria tulipa*)

to outer lip, but not on to siphonal canal; anterior tip of canal may have orange area.
Measures up to 3 inches in length.

Florida Horse Conch (*Pleuroploca gigantea*):
East and south-east coast U.S.A.; Mexico.
Occurs on lower shore and below, on sand.
Shell thick; very large body whorl; up to 9 whorls, usually knobbed but occasionally absent; spiral grooved; deeply sutured; elongated siphonal canal; very large oval aperture; inner lip smooth.
Exterior shell colour, greyish-white to brownish or salmon, with brown periostracum; aperture and inner lip margin, also siphonal canal, interior, orange-brown.
Measures up to 20 inches in length.

True Tulip (*Fasciolaria tulipa*):
East and south-east coast U.S.A.; West Indies.
Occurs on lower shore and below, in shallow water, on sand.
Shell thick; large body whorl; fine grooves; several finer grooves immediately below the deep suture; long siphonal canal; aperture narrow, long-oval.
Exterior shell colour, variable, ground colour, greenish-white or

173

brownish-yellow, mottled with blotches and streaks of greens, browns, yellows; aperture interior, plain ground colour.
Measures up to 6 inches in length.

TUN OR CASK SHELLS

These shells are thin, light, but strong. They occur in tropical water or warm shallow water in other regions. The mollusc is carnivorous, feeding on various other marine life and the adult when progressing is larger than the shell. It does not have an operculum to use, after withdrawing, to close its aperture.

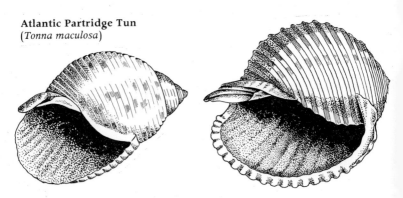

Atlantic Partridge Tun
(*Tonna maculosa*)

Giant Tun (*Tonna galea*)

Atlantic Partridge Tun (*Tonna maculosa*):
South-east coast U.S.A.; Caribbean; Brazil. A similar species is the **Partridge Tun** (*Tonna perdix*), which occurs in the west and south-west Pacific area.
Occurs on and below lower shore, in shallow water, in coral areas.
Shell rounded, with a large body whorl which has numerous fine spiral ridges; deep suture; wide, oval aperture; outer lip margin finely crenulated.
Exterior shell colour, brownish, with darker markings; aperture interior, tan.
Measures up to 4 inches in length.

Giant Tun (*Tonna galea*):
Mediterranean; south-east coast U.S.A.; Caribbean; Brazil; Pacific.
Occurs on lower shore and below, on sand; empty shells, due to their lightness, are often washed ashore.
Shell rounded, with a very large body whorl which has numerous flattened, spaced ridges; deep suture; short spire; very wide oval aperture; outer lip margin crenulated.
Exterior shell colour, pale brown.
Measures up to 7 inches in length.

OLIVE SHELLS

This is a large family, totalling several hundred, and is world-wide, chiefly in tropical regions. Their coloration and patterning is extremely variable and an interesting collection could specially consist solely of Olive Shells. They have several wrinkles and folds on the columella, but do not have an operculum. The molluscs are carnivorous on small molluscs and burrow in sand. To discover living specimens a search should be made during the night, at low tide or in shallow water, when they will be seen emerging to feed.

Lettered Olive (*Oliva sayana*):
South-east coast U.S.A.
Occurs on lower shore and below, in sand.
Shell glossy, has a large body whorl; whorl sides slightly concave; pointed apex; long, narrow aperture.
Exterior shell colour, variable, creamy-white, golden-yellow, greyish-tan, with a varying amount of irregular mottled brown markings, some of them appearing tent-like.
Measures up to $2\frac{1}{2}$ inches in length.

Netted Olive (*Oliva reticularis*):
South-east coast U.S.A.; Caribbean.
Occurs on lower shore and below, in sand.
Shell glossy, similar to Lettered Olive, but whorl sides more convex; also smaller.
Exterior shell colour, variable, rare plain white, usually criss-

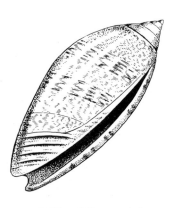

Lettered Olive (*Oliva sayana*)

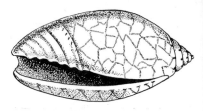

Netted Olive (*Oliva reticularis*)

Tent Olive (*Oliva porphyria*)

crossed with a brown network pattern; some examples may also have spiral brown bands on whorls.

Measures up to 2 inches in length.

Purple Dwarf Olive (*Olivella biplicata*):
Pacific coast Canada and U.S.A.
Occurs on lower shore.
Shell's glossy body whorl more bulbous than previous two Olives; aperture gapes wider; a callus on columella wall; small whorls and apex form a sharp point.
Exterior shell colour, variable, creamy or bluish-grey; base of shell aperture and body whorl, purple.
Measures up to an inch in length.

Tent Olive (*Oliva porphyria*)
Pacific coast Central America.
Occurs on lower shore and below, on sand.
Shell has a very large body whorl; small whorls and apex form a sharp point; long, narrow aperture; numerous folds on the columella.
Exterior shell colour, creamy-white and brown, except for creamy-white markings on body whorl which have a triangular, tent-like shape; aperture interior, creamy-white.
Measures up to 5 inches in length.

Plate XI The **Bat** or **Vesper Volute**
(*Aulica vespertilio*)

Plate XII The **Pacific Lettered Cone**
(*Conus litteratus*)

VOLUTE SHELLS

There are approximately two hundred species of Volute Shells. The majority of them occur in shallow, tropical water, although several of the North American species live in cooler, deep water. On the columella Volute Shells have several folds, while in most species the nuclear whorl is a small, knobbed, smooth structure. Some of the Volute molluscs have a very large foot, used to protectively cover part of the smooth, porcelain-like shell. The Volute molluscs are all carnivorous on small invertebrate sea creatures as prey. Some Volutes are rare or uncommon, thus valuable and are highly prized as specimens by collectors.

Bat or Vesper Volute (*Aulica vespertilio*):
Philippine Islands.
Occurs on lower shore and below.
Shell glossy, with a smooth, but finely striated surface; a large body whorl, with blunt knobs on the shoulder; apex flat-topped; four folds on the columella; short siphonal canal; large wide aperture.
Exterior shell colour, variable, pale greyish-green, pale brown or creamy-brown, with numerous irregular, zig-zag brown markings; base of columella orange or brownish; aperture white, whitish-blue or greenish, with a brown line around full extent of outer edge.
Measures up to 3 inches in length.

Junonia Volute (*Scaphella junonia*):
South-east coast U.S.A.; Gulf of Mexico.
Occurs on lower shore and below.
Shell glossy, smooth; a large body whorl, but no blunt knobs; apex more pointed; four folds on the columella; short siphonal canal; long, fairly narrow aperture; no operculum.
Exterior shell colour, cream or pale brown, with numerous spiral rows of rounded or almost square, purple to dark brown spots; base of columella white or pale brown; aperture the same.
Measures up to 5 inches in length.

Kiener's Volute (*Scaphella kieneri*):
South-east coast, U.S.A.; Gulf of Mexico.
Occurs in deep water.
Shell elongated, glossy, with a smooth, but finely striated surface; a large body whorl, but no blunt knobs; apex more pointed; large, long, narrow aperture; no operculum.
Exterior shell colour, pale creamy-tan or pale brownish-white, with up to 8 spiral rows of squared or rectangular chocolate-brown or reddish-brown spots on the whorls; base of columella is white; aperture white or creamy.
Measures up to 8 inches in length.

CONE SHELLS

Several of these familiar shells are sold by most shell shops. There are about 500 world species, living in warm and tropical water, usually among rocks and coral reefs. They are extremely variable in coloration and patterning. The living Cone molluscs are carnivorous, their prey being marine worms and other molluscs, occasionally fish. Their poison-injecting mechanism can cause a serious sting which has been known to be fatal to human beings, so Cones should be gathered and handled carefully, particularly at night when they are feeding actively. A coiled tube in the head supplies a neurotoxic venom to the proboscis where the radula tooth, like a miniature harpoon, plus the venom, is ejected into the victim. After ejection the radula tooth is not retrieved but is replaced in the proboscis mouth by another one ready for use. The horny operculum is long, narrow and shorter than the aperture length.

Alphabet Cone (*Conus spurius*)

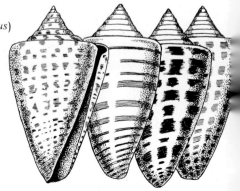

Alphabet Cone (*Conus spurius*):
South-east coast U.S.A.; Gulf of Mexico; Caribbean.
Occurs on lower shore and below, on sand.
Shell heavy; very large, broad at the top, but tapering body whorl; top whorls give a concave shape to pointed spire; whorl sides smooth; long, narrow aperture.
Exterior shell colour, variable, typically creamy-white with spiral rows of orange yellow and irregular, squarish blotches and spots; aperture, white; other forms have small paler spots, much larger spiral, purplish-brown, squarish blotches, or spiral, orange-brown or yellow bands.
Measures up to 3 inches in length.

Californian Cone (*Conus californicus*):
Pacific coast U.S.A.; Mexico.
Occurs on lower shore and below, among rocks.
Shell smooth and typical Cone-shaped, except that shoulders of body whorl are rounded so that the top whorls and spire 'blend', and there is less distinction where they meet the body whorl than in other Cones; aperture long, narrow.
Exterior shell colour, pale brown; aperture, similar.
Measures up to an inch in length.

Crown Cone (*Conus regius*)
South-east coast U.S.A.; West Indies.
Occurs on lower shore and below, on coral reefs.
Shell typical Cone-shape, but spire and top of body whorl is knobbed.
Exterior shell colour, variable, usually white with mottling of browns; occasionally all-brown without mottling; top of spire usually all-white.
Measures up to 3 inches in length.

Florida Cone (*Conus floridanus*):
East and south-east coast U.S.A.
Occurs on lower shore and below, on sand.
Shell typical Cone-shape, but tops of spire whorls are concave and so these whorls are pronounced at the suture.
Exterior shell colour, variable, typically white with large areas of yellow, orange, or brownish-orange, a white band on the body

179

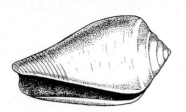

Californian Cone
(*Conus californicus*)

Crown Cone (*Conus regius*)

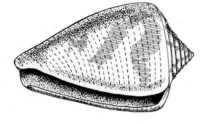

Interrupted Cone (*Conus ximenes*)

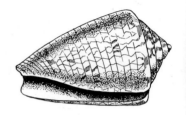

Lucid Cone (*Conus lucidus*)

whorl; other forms are darker with pale areas and rows of brown spots, or brown with darker lines.
Measures up to 2 inches in length.

Interrupted Cone (*Conus ximenes*):
Pacific coast Mexico, Central America; north-west coast South America.
Occurs on lower shore and below.
Shell typical Cone-shape, except shoulders of body whorl slightly rounded.
Exterior shell colour, greyish-white, with darker areas of greyish-blue or brown; body whorl has close spiral of darker dots and broken lines.
Measures up to 2 inches in length.

Lucid Cone (*Conus lucidus*):
Pacific coast Mexico, Central America; north-west coast South America.
Occurs on lower shore and below.
Shell typical Cone-shape.
Exterior shell colour, creamy-white; body whorl has brown pattern of lines which give it the appearance of being crazed;

180

smaller whorls have larger brown blotch markings, including shoulder of body whorl; aperture, whitish.
Measures up to 2 inches in length.

Pacific Lettered Cone (*Conus litteratus*):
Indo-Pacific area.
Occurs on lower shore and below, on sand, usually near coral reefs.
Shell heavy, very large, broad at top, but tapering body whorl; tops of whorls flat or slightly concave; spire flattened; body whorl smooth; long, narrow aperture.
Exterior shell colour, variable, creamy-white or brownish-white, with spiral rows of red-brown, dark brown, bluish grey-brown spots, blotches and semi-triangular shaped markings; top of whorls have irregular zebra-like red-brown and dark brown patterning; central spire area white, aperture, white.
Measures up to 5 inches in length.

TUSK OR TOOTH SHELLS

As their name describes, the shell shape is like an elephant's tusk, tubular and wider at the anterior end. They occur in shallow and deep water, on and in sand and mud, feeding upon microscopic marine life. The shells are tough despite their seeming frailty and occur cast up on the shore. These curious molluscs have no true head, gills, eyes or heart, the trilobed foot projecting from the anterior end, as water for respiration is indrawn and expelled through the narrow end held above the habitat. Species which occur on the Pacific coast were collected by American Indians to use as money for trading or to create jewellery and ornaments.

Common Elephant Tusk (*Dentalium entale*):
British Isles; west Europe.
Occurs below lower shore.
Shell slightly curved.
Exterior shell colour, white.
Measures up to 2 inches in length.
There is an American form of this species:

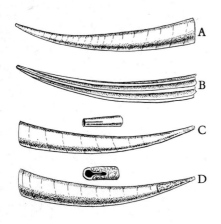

Tusk or Tooth Shells

A. Common Elephant Tusk
(*Dentalium entale*)

B. Panelled Tusk
(*Dentalium laqueatum*)

C. Ivory Tusk
(*Dentalium eboreum*)

D. Stimpsons Tusk
(*Dentalium entale stimpsoni*)

Stimpson's Tusk (*Dentalium entale stimpsoni*)
which occurs from Nova Scotia, Canada, to Massachusetts, U.S.A.,
it usually has the apex eroded and chalky.

Indian Money Tusk (*Dentalium pretiosum*):
Alaska; Pacific coast Canada, U.S.A., Mexico.
Occurs below lower shore.
Shell curved, plain; short notch on apex.
Exterior shell colour, white, with dull buff growth rings.
Measures up to 2 inches in length.

Ivory Tusk (*Dentalium eboreum*):
South-east coast U.S.A.; Caribbean.
Occurs on lower shore and below.
Shell glossy, curved to a fine apex, which has a narrow slit.
Exterior shell colour, ivory-white, but may have a pink tint.
Measures up to 2 inches in length.

Panelled Tusk (*Dentalium laqueatum*):
South-east coast U.S.A.; Caribbean.
Occurs below lower shore, on sand.
Shell curved, with up to 12 thick, longitudinal ribs and thin lines
between them.
Exterior shell colour, white.
Measures up to $2\frac{1}{2}$ inches in length.

Recommended for Further Reading

British Shells, by Nora F. McMillan (Warne)
Shell Life, by Edward Step (Warne)
Collecting Sea Shells, by F. D. Ommanney (Arco)
Pocket Guide to the Sea Shore, by John Barrett and C. M. Yonge (Collins)
Seashore Life In Colour, by Gwynne Vevers (Blandford)
Seashells of the World, by R. T. Abbott (Golden Press, New York)
Seashells of North America, by R. T. Abbott (Golden Press, New York)

Index

184

Grottie-Buckie, 137, 138

Hard-Shell Clams, 87, 88
Heart Clams or Shells, 61, 77
Heart Cockle, 78
Helmet Shells, 169: Emperor, 169, 170; Flame, 170; King, 170, 171; Prickly, 170, 171; Queen, 169, 170; Tuscan, 171, 172
Horn Shells, 141, 142
Horse Winkle, 157, 158
Hungarian Cap, 132, 133

Iceland Cyprina, 78

Jack-Knife Clams, 65, 66: Atlantic, 66; Californian, 66, 67; Green, 67
Janthina Snails, 149
John O' Groats, 137, 138

Kidney-Buckie, 150, 151

Lacuna Periwinkles, 127; Northern, 130
Lantern Shells, 108: Convex, 109; Papery, 109
Lima Shells, 51; *Lima glaciata*, 51; Rough, 51, 52; Spiny, 52
Limpets, 17, 24, 112, 113: anatomy of, 30, 31; Atlantic Plate, 113, 114; Blue-rayed, 113, 114; Blue-spotted, 113, 114; China, 114, 115; Common, 115; Fingered, 115, 116; Giant Owl, 115, 116; Great Keyhole, 116; Keyhole, 116, 117; Kingfisher, 113, 114; Linné's Puncturella, 117; Lister's Keyhole, 117; *Patella intermedia*, 117, 118; Rough, 118; Slit, 118; Tortoiseshell, 113, 114; Volcano, 118, 119; White Tortoiseshell, 118, 119
Littleneck Clam, 87, 88
Lucina or Lucines, 79: Californian, 79, 80; Florida, 79; Northern, 79, 80; Pennsylvanian, 80; Prickly, 81; Tiger, 80, 81
Lutraria magna, 105

Macoma Shells or Clams, 96: Atlantic Grooved, 97; Balthic, 93, 94, 97; Bent-nose, 97; Chalky, 97; White Sand, 98
Mangelia Shells, 160: *Mangelia attenuata*, 161; *Mangelia nebula*, 161
Mollusc anatomy, 27: Univalve, 27–31; Bivalve, 31–34
Moon Shells or Snails, 146: Common Northern, 148; Lewis', 147, 148
Murex Shells, 162: Apple, 162, 163; Eastern, 162, 164; Gem, 162 163; Giant Atlantic, 162, 164; Lace, 163; Pink-

mouthed, 163, 164; Purple Dye, 163, 164; Radix, 164; Ramose, 164
Mussels, 54: Bean Horse, 54, 55; Bearded Horse, 55; Blue, 54, 55; Common Edible, 54, 55; Hooked, 54, 56; Horse, 54, 56; Northern Horse, 54, 56; Mediterranean, 56; Tulip, 56, 57

Nassa Mud Snails, 154: Common Eastern, 155; Eastern Mud, 155; Giant Western, 155, 156; Western, 156, 157
Natica Shells, 146: Colourful Atlantic, 147
Necklace Shells, 146: Common, 147, 148; Large, 147, 148
Needle Shell, 140, 142
Needle Whelk, 140, 142
Neptune Shells: New England, 151, 152; North-West, 152
Nerite Shells, 126: Bleeding Tooth, 126; Four-toothed, 126, 127
Nun, 137, 138

Olive Shells, 175: Lettered, 175, 176; Netted, 175, 176; Purple Dwarf, 176; Tent, 176
Ormer, 111, 112; Pink, 112; Red, 112
Otter Shells, 104: Common, 104, 105; *Lutraria magna*, 105
Oysters, 35: American Blue Point, 35, 36, 37; Eastern, 35, 37; Edible, Flat, Native English or European, 35, 36; Native Pacific, 36, 37; Portuguese, 36–38; Pearl Oysters, 38: Atlantic, 38: 39; Black-lip, 38; Ceylon, 38, 39; Golden-lip or Pearl Button, 39; Japanese, 39
Thorny Oysters, 40: Atlantic, 40; Pacific, 40
Wing Oysters, 38, 41: Atlantic 41; Western, 41; Wing or Wing-shell, 42
Saddle Oysters, Jingle Shells, 42: Common, Atlantic Jingle, 42, 43; *Heteranomia squamula*, 42, 43; Ribbed Saddle, 43; Saddle, Silver Shell, 43, 44

Pacific Chinese Hat, 134
Pandora Shells or Clams, 107: Gould's, 107; *Pandora pinna*, 108
Pectens, 44
Pelican's Foot Shell, 145, 146; American, 145
Pen Shells, 52: Amber, 53; Giant Mediterranean, 53, 54
Periwinkles, 22, 127: Checkered, 127, 128; Common Edible, 127, 128; Eroded, 128; European, 128; Flat, 128, 129; Northern Rough, 129, 130; Northern Yellow, 128, 129; Rough, 129, 130; Small, 129, 130

Piddocks, 68, 69; American, 69, 70; Common, 70; Great, 72, 73; Little 71; Oval, 72, 73; Paper, 72; Red-Nose, 72–73; White, 72, 73; Wood, 73

Pinna, 52

Purple, 157, 158

Purpuras, 157: Foliated Thorn, 159

Quahogs, 87: Northern, 87, 88; Southern, 88

Razor Clam, 65, 66

Razor Shells, 17, 32, 65, 66: *Ensis arcuatus*, 67; Grooved, 66, 67; Pod, 66, 67; Sword, 66, 68; Transparent, 66, 68

Reversed Horn Shell, 141, 142

Rock Borer, 71: Wrinkled, 73, 74

Round Clam, 87, 88

Scallops, 44: Atlantic Bay, 44; Calico, 45, 46; Giant Pacific, 45, 46; Giant Rock, 45, 46; Great, Edible, Clam, 45, 46, 47; Hunchback, 46–48; Jacob's, 47, 48; Kelp-weed, 47; Lion's-paw, 47, 48; Mediterranean, 47, 48; Queen, Quin, 47, 48; San Diego, 48, 49; Seven-rayed, 49, 50; Tiger, 49, 50; Variegated, 49, 50; Zig-zag, 50

Screw-shell, 144, 145

Sea-Ear, 111, 112

Sea Pens, 52

Shells with tall spires, 140

Shore Types, 19, 20: Shingle, 19; Sandy, 19; Muddy sand or Mud, 19, 20; Rocky shores and Shore Pool, 20

Shore Zones, divisions of, 18, 19: Supra-littoral or Upper, 18; Splash or Spray, 18; Mid-littoral or Middle, 18, 19; Sub-littoral or Lower, 18, 19

Slipper Limpets, 132: American Slipper, 132; Onyx, 134

Slipper Shells: Atlantic, 132; Spiny, 135; Western White, 135

Soft-Shell Clams, 105, 106: Truncate, 105, 106

Spindle Shells, 160: Prickly, 160, 161; Ribbed, 160, 161

Spiny Slipper Shell, 135

Staircase Shells, 131, 142

Stick-Farthing, 137, 138

Sting Winkle, 159; Small, 159

Striate Cup-and-Saucer Shell, 135

Sundial Shells, 131: Common Atlantic, 131

Sunset Shells or Clams, 99, 100; Cali-fornian, 100, 101; Faroe, 100, 101; Large, 100; Ribbed, 101; Tellin-like, 101

Surf Clams, 102: Atlantic, 102, 104

Tellin, 32, 92: Baltic, 93, 94; Bean-like, 93; Blunt, 93; Candy-stick, 93, 94; Donax-like, 94; Hatchet, 94; Little, 94, 95; Rose-petal, 95; Rough, 95; Salmon, 95; Speckled, 95; Sunrise, 96; Thin, 96

Thracia Shells, 108: Common Pacific, 108; Conrad's, 108, 109

Tooth Shells, 181

Top Shells, 119: *Calliostoma papillosum*, 119, 120; *Cantharidus exaspertus*, 120; Channelled, 120; Common, 123, 124; Flat, 120; *Gibbula magus*, 121, 122; *Gibbula pennanti*, 121; *Gibbula varie-gata*, 122; Greenland Margarite, 121, 122; Grey, 121, 122; Grooved, 122, 123; Painted, 123, 124; Purple, 120, 122; Ribbed, 123; 'Silver Tommy', 121, 122; Speckled Tegula, 123, 124; Thick, 124; 'Toothed Winkle', 124; West Indian, 124, 125

Tower Shell, 144, 145

Triton Shells, 165: Angular, 165; Atlantic, 165, 166; Common Hairy, 165; Knobbed, 166; Knobbed Triton's Trumpet, 166; Triton's Trumpet, 165, 166

Trivias, 135: Atlantic Coffee Bean, 136; Californian, 137

Trophon Shells, 160: Orpheus, 160

Trough Shells, 102: Cut, 102, 104; Elliptical, 102, 103; Glaucous, 103; Rayed, 103, 104; Thick, 103, 104

Tulip Conches, 172

Tulip Shells, 172: Banded, 172, 173; True, 173, 174

Tun Shells, 174: Atlantic Partridge, 174; Partridge, 174; Giant, 174, 175

Turban Shells, 125: Chestnut, 125; Green, 125; Gold-mouthed, 125, 126

Tusk Shells, 181: Common Elephant, 181; Indian Money, 182; Ivory, 182; Panelled, 182; Stimpson's, 182

Venus Shells or Clams, 83: Banded, 83, 84; Cross-barred, 84; European, 86; King, 84; Oval, 84, 85; Pacific White, 85; Pale, 85; Rock, 90; Royal Comb, 85, 86; Striped, 85, 86; Sunray, 86; Warty, 86, 87

Violet Sea Snails, 149

Volute Shells, 177: Bat, 177; Junonia, 177; Kiener's, 178; Vesper, 177

Wedge Shells, 91: Banded, 91, 92

Wentletraps, 142: Brown-banded, 142, 143; Common, 142, 143; Greenland, 143; Money, 143; Turton's, 143, 144; Wroblewski's, 144

Western White Slipper Shell, 135